A Wilderness Zone

A Wilderness Zone

and Other Essays

WALTER BRUEGGEMANN

CASCADE *Books* · Eugene, Oregon

A WILDERNESS ZONE
And Other Essays

Cascade Books
An Imprint of Wipf and Stock Publishers
199 W. 8th Ave., Suite 3
Eugene, OR 97401

www.wipfandstock.com

PAPERBACK ISBN: 978-1-6667-0123-4
HARDCOVER ISBN: 978-1-6667-0124-1
EBOOK ISBN: 978-1-6667-0125-8

Cataloguing-in-Publication data:

Names: Brueggemann, Walter, author.

Title: A wilderness zone : and other essays / Walter Brueggemann.

Description: Eugene, OR: Cascade Books, 2021. | Includes bibliographical references and indexes.

Identifiers: ISBN 978-1-6667-0123-4 (paperback). | ISBN 978-1-6667-0124-1 (hardcover). | ISBN 978-1-6667-0125-8 (ebook).

Subjects: LCSH: Bible—Criticism, interpretation, etc. | Bible—Homiletical use. | Political theology.

Classification: BS1191.5 B750 2021 (print). | BS1191.5 (ebook).

10/04/21

Contents

Preface

THE SEVERAL PIECES IN this volume have been written in response to the generous invitation of Mary Brown to contribute to her blog platform, church.anew. I promptly seized upon her invitation and have spent an intense year of making regular contributions to her blog. I am grateful to Mary for her suggestive, visionary leadership. Her blog of course continues, now that I have completed my contributions to it.

The chance to write brief ad hoc scripture expositions for a blog platform is a most welcome opportunity for an old, weary interpreter who no longer has the stamina to do extended work. In these several pieces I have worked to trace out possible interfaces between specific scripture references and matters at the forefront of our common social life. It is my hunch that, almost without fail, such an interface creates a very different angle of vision for any element of our common social life, because it situates such a topic in the context of the biblical narrative that is occupied by the holy agency of God. Such an alternative angle of vision helps to defamiliarize us from our usual discernment according to the master narrative of democratic capitalism that is most widely shared across the spectrum of conservatives and progressives. Because our common angle of vision shared by progressives and conservatives has a very low ceiling of human ultimacy, we (all of us!) easily come to think that our particular reading of social reality is absolute and beyond question, even if dominated by a tacit ideology. It is my bet that an interface with biblical testimony can and will deabsolutize our excessive certitude and permit us to look again at the social "facts" that are in front of us. I do not think and do not suggest that such interfaces with scripture are inevitable; they are rather suggestive, impressionistic, and fleeting, the kind of linkage that is available in the matrix of faith that is not fixed on certitude.

It is my hope that readers of these brief pieces will find them suggestive in a way that helps us look again and see again. In any case, this writing has suited me well, as I no longer have the energy or interest to do the hard critical work upon which good serious faith depends. For that reason I am glad to acknowledge the host of critical scholars who have done the hard work on which I depend. I am also glad to acknowledge the hard sustained work of many practical scripture interpreters—teachers and pastors—who continue, along with me, to seek for the emancipatory connections between scripture and life.

I am glad, yet again, to express my continuing and abiding thanks to K.C. Hanson and Cascade Books for willingness to publish these pieces. I am grateful for K.C.'s careful, discerning, quick work that so frequently brings my work to fruition.

Walter Brueggemann
Columbia Theological Seminary
August 11, 2021

1

A Wilderness Zone

THE NARRATIVE OF FAITH is characteristically about a journey in and through the wilderness. That theme seems particularly pertinent among us now in our present social crisis. We are "into the wilderness" as so many of our old social certitudes are now in acute jeopardy. (I write this on the day of the funeral in Houston for George Floyd who was murdered by police in Minneapolis.)[1] That crisis is deep, thick, and complex, but it has three faces of presentation:

- the virus that for now has outflanked our scientific capacity;

- the economic meltdown in the wake of the virus; and

- a skewed criminal justice system for which police misconduct is the visible front.

These three dimensions of the crisis together have a huge impact on the body politic:

- the virus leaves us variously *vulnerable* in its not yet understood danger;

---

1. This essay was originally written as a new introduction to the second edition of my book, *Journey to the Common Good*.

- the economic meltdown leaves many people in deep *dislocation*; and

- the crisis in criminal justice evokes *anger and fear.*

When I thought about these poignant social realities of *vulnerability, dislocation,* plus *fear and anger,* it occurred to me that in the Bible the context that presents a like lived experience is the wilderness sojourn of Israel after the slaves had departed Pharaoh's Egypt. Thus, I suggest that in the face of our crisis we may do well to consider the wilderness tradition in the Bible as a context in which faith may be powerfully pertinent. We in our current circumstance have an opportunity to bring that tradition close to our own experience. That narrative, I suggest, is marked by three remembered realities.

Escape to the wilderness from Egypt meant that Israel had moved *beyond the reach and governance of Pharaoh.* His control did not extend to that untamed territory. This meant for the newly emancipated slaves that they freed, at last, from the coercive demands of Pharaoh that served his hunger for a monopoly grain.[2] Pharaoh's requirements were unending and insatiable (see Exod 5), and now the slaves no longer had to answer for unreasonable brick quotas, a harbinger first of unreasonable quotas for chopping cotton and now unreasonable requirements for meat-packing workers! It is no wonder that just as the slaves crossed the waters into the wilderness away from the reach of Pharaoh's demand economy that Miriam and the other women took tambourines, danced, and sang:

> Sing to the LORD, for he has triumphed gloriously;
> horse and rider he has thrown into the sea. (Exod 15:21)

Their action was the performance of bodily freedom, for their bodies had long ached with unbearable work. As I pondered their song and dance of freedom, I noted the contemporary parallel as

---

2. See Gen 47:13–26; and Scott, *Against the Grain.*

the protestors danced in the streets in DC where the huge yellow letters spelled out, "Black Lives Matter." It was as though the protestors sensed that they had, at least for now, escaped and moved beyond the coercive fear and greed of the predatory economy of US patriarchal capitalism. That dance, like that of the earlier dance of Miriam, gave bodily articulation for bodies now permitted their full joyous freedom, even if under the all-seeing eye of Pharaoh's surveillance.

At the same time, however, a move beyond the reach and governance of Pharaoh meant that the erstwhile slaves could no longer count on the certitudes and predictabilities of Pharaoh; as a result the wilderness felt like a free-fall into risk. Without Pharaoh's jobs, how will we pay the rent? It is for that reason that as soon as the slaves crossed out of Exodus 15 and Egypt into Exodus 16 and the wilderness, in that moment they wished for a prompt return to Pharaoh, ready to trade-off their newly found freedom for the certitude of Pharaoh's bread supply:

> If only we had died by the hand of the LORD in the land of Egypt, when we sat by the fleshpots and ate our fill of bread; for you have brought us out into this wilderness to kill this whole assembly with hunger. (Exod 16:3)

Our circumstance is like that now as the loss of Pharaoh's jobs generates great risk. Wilderness evokes great soberness and a wish for return to the way it was "back there." The wilderness marked by great joy can readily enough turn to anxiety and nostalgia for the old security:

> If only we had meat to eat! We remember the fish we used to eat in Egypt for nothing, the cucumbers, the melons, the leeks, the onions, and the garlic; but now our strength is dried up, and there is nothing at all but his manna to look at. (Num 11:4–5)

Some soon wearied of their new circumstance and wished for the regularities of the old system of coercion. I suppose the contemporary appeal to "law and order" is designed to call attention to the fact that *emancipation* for some feels like *anarchy* to others.

The wilderness is a new liminal environment that requires fresh constructive thinking and action. So now in the moment of emancipated bodies, the wilderness requires hard thinking and bold action for the sake of an alternative social apparatus. It is one thing to cross the water into freedom. It is quite another thing to morph from the dance of freedom to a viable shared life there. In the memory of ancient Israel that is the burden of the wilderness-like moment of exile when Israel a new world now void of city, king, and temple:

> Build houses and live in them; plant gardens and eat what they produce. Take wives and have sons and daughters; take wives for your sons, and give your daughters in marriage, that they may have sons and daughters; multiply there, and do not decrease. (Jer 29:5–6)

The prophetic tradition of Israel exhibits poetic-prophetic efforts at such imagination outside the sphere of the coercive regime of Jerusalem and beyond the reach of imperial Babylon, a stand-in for Pharaoh. Thus Isaiah can imagine a new alternative city (Isa 65:17–25). Jeremiah can evoke a new grace-laden covenant (Jer 31:31–34). And Ezekiel can sketch out a new symmetrical city with abiding holiness at its center (Ezek 48:1–35). Actual social reality may take the form of none of these poetic offers, but the wilderness inhabitants cannot short-cut the imaginative efforts that run beyond anything thinkable or imaginable amid the coercion of Pharaoh. (It is for the same reason that Jesus told parables, acts of imagination beyond administered reality in the Roman Empire). It is the work to be done after the first flush of dancing in order to be sure that there is no reembrace of Pharaoh, because Pharaoh, despite all hopes, has not and will not change. Pharaoh will continue to be coercive and predatory. Wilderness is the hard work of alternative!

≈

Pharaoh's monopoly of grain assured that there as in Egypt a steady supply of food. In contrast to Pharaoh's Egypt, *the wilderness is a place without visible life-supports.* While the Israelites were eager to escape Egypt, they inescapably found the wilderness to be a place bereft of life's sustenance—bread, meat, water. It did not take long to discover that they faced in the wilderness a most precarious existence. Some promptly yearned for a return to Egypt. Even though they had known harsh oppression there, what they remembered about Egypt, rather than oppression, was a reliable food supply:

> Why is the LORD bringing us into this land to fall by the sword? Our wives and our little ones will become booty; would it not b better for us to go back to Egypt?" So they said to one another, "Let us choose a captain and go back to Egypt." (Num 14:3–4)

There was a sustained complaint against the leadership of Moses, for he was not able to guarantee a food supply in the way that Pharaoh had. The wilderness left the freed slaves with an option, so it seemed to them, of death or resubmissions to Pharaoh's Egypt. Of course it is like that amid the virus in which we face an awareness that an income necessary for life can be had only with the participation in the capitalist economic system. Thus the "reopening of the economy" in some ways is not unlike a return to Egypt, a readiness to risk the virus for the sake of livability.

In the wilderness material of the Bible we are offered two narratives that attest that the wilderness, presided over by the generous creator God, does indeed contain viable life supports, even though they are not easily visible, and even though they do not take conventional form. In the more familiar account of Exodus 16, the complaint is against the leadership of Moses. Moses, however, deflects the complaint away from himself and on to YHWH (v.\ 7). In response to the complaint of Israel, it is remembered that YHWH heard the complaint and responded with great gifts of food. First there came quail to supply meat (v. 13). And then there was bread; it was a "fine flakey substance as fine as frost on the ground" (v. 14). That gift of bread was not something they recognized. They asked about its identity: "What is it?" (*man-hu*) (v. 15). That question became the name of the new bread, so that *man-hu* morphed to *manna*. The peculiar name for the peculiar bread of the wilderness was the consequence of an unanswered wonderment. "What it is" is gift bread that escapes all conventional expectations and that defies all conventional explanations. The "wonder" of the bread is that wilderness turns out to a place of ample bread!

> Gather as much of it as each of you needs, an omer to a person according to the number of persons, all providing for those in their own tents. The Israelites did so, some gathering more, some less. But they measured it with an omer, those who had gatherer much had nothing over, and those who gatherer little had no shortage; they gathered as much as each of them needed. (vv. 16–18)

Divinely given abundance is the response to crisis complaint! That strange gift is amplified in the next chapter. Now there is no water, for wilderness is an arid place (Exod 17:2). Again there is complaint against the leadership of Moses. Again Moses deflects the complaint from himself to the Lord. Again the Lord responds in a way beyond expectation:

> Strike the rock, and water will come out of it, so that the people may drink. (17:6)

Water from rock" is not unlike "blood from a turnip"! It turns out that the wilderness is a place of ample water. Thus Israel receives, beyond any explanation and outside the delivery system of Pharaoh, the necessities of meat, bread, and water. The wilderness where YHWH presides turns teems with viable life supports that become visible by the inscrutable gift of the God of abundance.

A second narrative reflects the same wilderness crisis. In Numbers 11 Israel is again desperate for food, this time fatigued with the manna that had become excessively familiar to them. This time, however, Moses refuses to be YHWH's advocate. He sides with the complaining Israelites against YHWH:

> Why have you treated your servant so badly? Why have I not found favor in your sight, that you lay the burden of all this people on me? Did I conceive all this people? Did I give birth to them that you should say to me, 'Carry them in your bosom, as a nurse carries a sucking child,'

> to the land that you promised on oath to their ancestors? Where am I to get meat to give to all this people? For they come weeping to me and say, "Give us meat to eat!" I am not able to carry all this people alone, for they are too heavy for me. If this is the way you are going to treat me, put me to death at once—if I have found favor in your sight—and do not let me see my misery. (Num 11:11–15)

Moses has had more than enough of the responsibility in his impossible leadership role. He voices the sense that he has not received adequate backup from God. YHWH responds to Moses' desperate demand:

> Therefore the LORD will give you meat, and you shall eat. You shall eat not only one day, or two days, or five days, or ten days, or twenty days, but for a whole month—until it comes out of your nostrils, and become loathsome to you—because you have rejected the Lord who is among you and have wailed b before him, saying, "Why did we ever leave Egypt?" (vv. 18–20)

That divine response is not generous and gracious. As Moses is fed up with Israel's complaints, so YHWH is fed up with the complaints of Israel and Moses. YHWH promises ample meat, but makes the promise in a fit of anger so that the promised meat will be the cause of respiratory problems perhaps not unlike the virus. Indeed the threat of YHWH is strong enough that we might expect a desperate response from Israel with too many quail, "I can't breathe!" The narrative ends with an ample gift of quail that had been promised:

> Then the wind went out from the LORD, and it brought quails from the sea and let them fall beside the camp, about a day's journey on the other side, all around the camp, about two cubits deep on the ground. So the people worked all that day and night and all the next day, gathering the quails. (vv. 31–32)

It was a gift from God marked by divine anger that ended in strife and destruction.

It is not difficult to imagine a like outcome of the protests concerning police misconduct. One can imagine a *quail-fight* among leaders with a delay in any real social gains. It turns out that the wilderness of protest is laden with gifts. But those gifts cannot be easily converted into any familiar social form. The food crisis in the wilderness required the articulation of newly imagined forms of common life. In this case the newly imagined form of Israel's common life is the Sabbath (Exod 16:22–26). The regular observance of Sabbath is acknowledgement that Israel is on the receiving end of life's sustenance. Israel does not possess or generate such sustenance, but receives it as a gift. And when Israel subsequently defiles Sabbath for the sake commerce, big trouble is sure to come (see Amos 8:4–6). Thus the generous food supply of the wilderness cannot be accommodated to the predatory practices of Pharaoh, for the food hoarded will melt, get worms, and smell badly (Exod 16:20–21). A failure of faithful imagination could cause Israel from the wilderness to replicate the economy and social practices of Pharaoh. So now among us a failure of imagination might lead to a replication of the old forms of our common life that bring with them conventional practices of exploitation, predation, and abuse. It is not easy to maintain alternative in the practice of real life economy. That, nevertheless, is the mandate of Moses and every community that wants to order life apart from Pharaoh's drama of oppression. The wilderness gifts of sustenance require "a more excellent way." This immense challenge for those who refuse Pharaoh's way is to continue to imagine, invent, and devise transformative ways to be together in the world. Eventually the wilderness people arrive at Sinai. There they will receive ten mandates as alternative to Pharaoh (Exod 20:1–17). The mandates concern *the holiness of God* that de-absolutizes everything else and the *centrality of the neighbor*. It is clear from Sinai and thereafter that these mandates contradict Pharaoh, for Pharaoh defied the holiness of God and dismissed the centrality of the neighbor. Wilderness food comes with built-in requirements. The challenge for Israel was to move out of wilderness into the land of promise and there to continue the disciplines of wilderness in the midst of storable crops:

> The manna ceased on the day they ate the produce of the
> land, and the Israelites no longer had manna; they ate the
> crops of the land of Canaan that year. (Josh 5:12)

The challenge now is to practice *manna-life* in an environment
of guaranteed harvest crops. As Scott has shows, the capacity to
store grain (or other kinds of commodity wealth) can readily lead
to *storage, surplus,* and concomitant *subsistence,* and the violence
necessary to maintain the unequal interface. When the memory of
wilderness fades and wilderness trust and gratitude are not urgent,
the prospect for genuine social alternative readily descends into
the "same old, same old."

≈

Pharaoh kept a tight lid on protest and complaint. No complaint in
the brickyard . . . or in the meat-packing job . . . or in prison . . . or
in a nursing home! Pharaoh requires that we simply suck it up and
keep moving, whereby our silence offers tacit assent to the rule of
Pharaoh. But of course the censoring of protest and complaint can
last only so long. Eventually all hell will break loose:

> After a long time the king of Egypt died. The Israelites
> groaned under their slavery and cried out. (Exod 2:23)

When their grievance breaks loose, there is no limit to its scope
and no limit to the danger such loudness poses for oppressive
power.

It is not surprising that when Israel arrived in the wilderness
it was completely prepared to "murmur." It is clear that *the wilderness is a venue for loud, legitimate protest in anger, impatience,
demand, and hope.* Of course, much of the protest in the wilderness is a response to present circumstance in the wilderness with
a scarcity of meat, bread, and water. But we may imagine as well,
however, that the protest of murmuring is more vigorous because
of the long silencing imposed by Pharaoh. It is as though Israel in
the wilderness, like a young child, has just learned a new sound of
her voice, and is sure to use it repeatedly. The wilderness is a place

that evokes, permits, and hosts loud protests that makes demands we had been taught by Pharaoh to deny. For that reason, the wilderness narrative is filled with persistent protest:

> And the people *complained* against Moses, saying, "What shall we drink?" (Exod 15:24)

> In the morning you shall see the glory of the LORD, because he has heard your *complaining* against the LORD. For what are we, that you *complain* against us?" And Moses said, "When the LORD gives you meat to eat in the evening and you fill of bread in the morning, because the LORD has heard the *complaining* that you utter against him—what are we?" Your *complaining* is not against us but against the LORD." (Exod 16:7–8)

> But the people thirsted there for water; and the people *complained* against Moses and said, "Why did you bring us out of Egypt to kill us and our children and livestock with thirst?" (Exod 17:3)

> How long shall this wicked congregation *complain* against me? I have heard the complaints of the Israelites which they *complain* against me . . . your dead bodies shall fall in this very wilderness; and of all your number, included in the census . . . who have *complained* against me. (Num 14:27, 29)

They are an unhappy bunch in the wilderness!

The wonder of the narrative is that the complaints are heard, taken seriously, and given a response. Thus Israel's protests are variously answered by God with meat, bread, and water. It turns out that the wilderness is a place of heavy-duty dialogic engagement in which the One with authority is attentive to and responsive to the needs and requirements of the vulnerable ones. This engagement between *authority and vulnerability* is an astonishing reality in the wilderness. This is so unlike Pharaoh in Egypt who in hardheartedness never heard a complaint and in harshness dismissed any voicing of groan from below.

In our season of wilderness reality with the virus, the economic crisis, and the pandemic of police misconduct, it is remarkable that we have arrived at vigorous, out-loud protest. All sorts of people are finally finding their voice; all sorts of people are hoping and insisting in solidarity with those who face the ominous realities of repression, brutality, and abandonment. This out-loud self-declaration from below is a new social reality among us. There can be no more top-down silencing that Pharaoh had perfected. It remains to be seen whether top-down civic authority can recognize this wilderness moment with a readiness for serious dialogic engagement, or whether we may expect more Pharonic silencing and abdication. In the wilderness narrative we get a fresh glimpse of God who now is known to be the one who can be effectively engaged "from below." It may be that we will get a new glimpse of social power among us, power that can effectively respond to out-loud self-announcement. The wilderness is not and cannot be a place of silence or silencing. It is rather a venue for protest, for acknowledged need, and for hope. The protesters around us are not acting out of cynicism or despair; they are acting in hope of transformative outcomes, just as Israel in the wilderness hoped for newness from the God to whom they protested.

Eventually the people of promise arrived at the land of promise. But the journey there is wilderness-laden. It remains to be seen whether in our time and place we will have the stamina and courage for a wilderness-laden enterprise of insistent hope, The wonder of wilderness is that there the erstwhile slaves encountered a God willing and able to engage with them, all so unlike their life with Pharaoh!

The faith of a wilderness people has entered Christian liturgy in the familiar hymn of William Williams:

> Guide me, O thou great Jehovah,
> pilgrim through this barren land.
> I am weak, but thou art mighty,
> hold me with thy powerful hand.
> Bread of heaven, bread of heaven,
> Feed me till I want no more;
> feed me till I want no more.
> Open now the crystal fountain,
> whence the healing stream doth flow.

Let the fire and cloudy pillar
led me all my journey through.
Strong deliverer, strong deliverer,
be thou still my strength and shield,
be thou still my strength and shield.
When I tread the verge of Jordan,
bid my anxious fears subside.
Death of death, and hell's destruction,
land me safe on Canaan's side.
Songs of praises, songs of praises
I will ever give to thee;
I will ever give to thee.[3]

The hymn acknowledges a wilderness condition of weakness and vulnerability; that weakness and vulnerability of course are countered by trusting affirmation in the might, power, and fidelity of the God who governs the wilderness. It is this God who will give bread.

The second stanza imagines the reliable guidance of God in places of risk and exposure by "fire and cloudy pillar," never doubting that God is present and reliable (see Exod 13:21). The third stanza features arrival at the place and land of promise marked by the boundary of the Jordan River. Thus the hymn echoes the cadences of hope and food, of risk and confidence, of threat and arrival. We are now in such a wilderness time when the old certitudes of Pharaoh are exposed as false, but when the arrival in a new placed of wellbeing is only an anticipation. We are in-between; that of course is where faith has a chance to make a decisive difference, confident that the God faithfulness gives new goodness. It is a conviction verified in the wilderness sojourn of Jesus. He was tempted when the force of evil tried to talk him out of his vocation. Then we are told:

Suddenly angels came and waited on him. (Matt 4:11)

It turns out that the wilderness, contrary to our fear and our conventional expectations, is securely governed by God who dispatches angels of mercy at points of need among the faithful.

3. "Guide Me, O Thou Great Jehovah," in *Glory to God*, 65.

While it may take Pharaoh time to realize it, we have in our society, departed Egypt. We are not yet at a new place of wellbeing. Being on the way, as we are, is hazardous. That risky way, however, is fully within the governing orbit of the faithful God. That conviction gives us courage to depart Pharaoh, readiness to receive new gifts that we cannot see, and freedom for loud articulation of hope-filled hurt and grief.

2

Abandoned!

THE VIRUS HAS CAUSED many people to *feel abandoned*. Beyond that the virus has caused many people in actuality to *be abandoned*. Consequently I have thinking about biblical articulations of a season of abandonment. To be sure these abandonments are not on the scale of being God-abandoned, but they no doubt move in the same sphere, so that the raise the issue of being *God-abandoned*. We are all familiar with Jesus' cry of abandonment on the cross:

> "Eli, Eli, lema sabachthani?" that is,
> "My God, my God,
> why have you *forsaken* me?" (Matt 27:46; Mark 15:34)

Of this cry, Jürgen Moltmann can conclude,

> According to Paul and Mark, Jesus himself was *abandoned* by this very God, his Father, and died with a cry of *godforsakenness*.[1]

We are, moreover, all familiar with the fact that Jesus was quoting from the Psalm of lament:

> My God, my God,
>   why have you *forsaken* me? (Ps 22:1)

1. Moltmann, *The Crucified God*, 241.

It is this unresolved utterance of abandonment at the center of the gospel narrative that of course creates a deep problematic for any pastor. I know of two common attempts to soften this cry of abandonment. First, it is worth notice that Psalm 22 moves at the end to a great assurance and affirmation:

> From the horns of the wild oxen you have rescued me.
> I will tell of your name to my brothers and sisters;
>> in the midst of the midst of the congregation I will
>> praise you. (vv. 21–22)

It is possible that Jesus implied the entire Psalm, speaking not only of abandonment but also of God's rescue. As a result, abandonment on the lips of Jesus is not the final word. Second and a less compelling softening of the cry is the notion that that the psalmist "felt" abandoned but was in fact not abandoned. But of course that is not what the psalmist said nor is it a helpful pastoral response for those who know themselves to be abandoned.

Much theology is marked by the conviction that God, along with being omnipotent and omniscient, is also *omnipresent*, that is, never absent. And of course if never absent, then the cry of Jesus or of the psalmist cannot be taken at face value. (The best critical affirmation of divine omnipresence known to me is the recent discussion by Katherine Sonderegger.[2] Sonderegger places a primary accent on the "hiddenness of God."[3])

Such a claim of hidden presence has a strong appeal for us. But against such a claim are both the attestation of scripture and the lived reality of peoples' lives. Thus I judge that we must allow for the genuine experience of divine absence and the real experience of being abandoned. Any assurance that flies in the face of that lived reality is not likely to be compelling or reassuring. In my judgment, we do better, theologically and pastorally, to acknowledge God's abandonment in our lives. In our life time surely the Nazi holocaust is an exhibit of divine abandonment that was lived through and known to be acutely real.

2. Sonderegger, *Systematic Theology*, 1:49–147.
3. See especially Isa 45:15; also Buber, *The Eclipse of God*.

If we linger over the interpretation that Israel (or even Jesus!) "felt" abandoned but was not really abandoned, we may notice the remarkable text of Isaiah 54:7–8 at the far edge of the exile:

> For a brief moment I *abandoned* you,
>> but with great compassion I will gather you.
> In overflowing wrath for a moment I *hid my face* from you,
>> but with everlasting love I will have compassion on you,
>> says the LORD, your Redeemer.

We have seen the voicing of abandonment by Israel and then by Jesus. But now this is, according to Isaiah, the voice of God's own self. This is God's own declaration of abandonment! In the first line of each of these verses, the poet offers a divine assertion of abandonment. The lines speak amid exile and declare the exile as a season of abandonment. (I will comment another time on the second lines of each of these verses). The first two lines, on the lips of God, assert that the Lord of the covenant has indeed abandoned covenant with Israel. These lines are an echo of God's declaration in Hosea:

> Then the LORD said, "Name him Lo-ammi, for you are
> not my people and I am not your God. (Hos 1:8)

This is the undoing of Israel's covenantal identity. The exile is characterized as the historical reality of that undoing. The abandonment is said to occur because of God's anger and loss of patience with Israel's recalcitrance. Perhaps it might be judged that God is whimsical or capricious about covenantal commitment to Israel, but that is not likely on the horizon of the poet.

The divine asseveration is stark and uninflected. It is eased and relieved to some extent by the reassurance of the second line of each verse; that assurance however does not change the stark harshness of the first line of each verse that had to be faced by the generation of the exile. *Compassion later* does not much change *abandonment now!*

So let us entertain the claim—pastorally, theologically, historically—that Israel in exile was indeed God-abandoned (and that Jesus on the cross reiterated and replicated the abandonment of Israel). This claim, I submit, is pastorally useful amid the virus, because it recognizes honestly and takes seriously the lived reality of those who die without the presence of loved ones, those who are left economically bereft, and those who mandated to continue to work in unsafe environments.

The summons of faith amid abandonment, I submit, is that we should in such circumstance maintain, with intentional resolve, faithful practices and disciplines that belong to our baptism. (Those who do not do so in ancient Israel, we may imagine, evaporated from the covenant community in despair). There is, however, an antidote to despair in the regular practices of the disciplines of faith. It does not seem a far stretch to imagine that these practices that fend off despair include at least the following:

1. In seasons of abandonment *people of faith tell sustaining stories.* In ancient Israel they told *the big stories* of YHWH's faithfulness, accounts of deliverance and transformation. These are the stories that evoked the characteristic mantra of wonder in Israel:

> For his steadfast love endures forever. (Ps 136:1, 2, 3, et al.)

These inexplicable actions of YHWH, not generic but one-time acts, are regarded as in Israel as "wonderful works" that defy explanation (see Ps 107:8, 15, 21, 31). But Israel also told *little stories* of fidelity:

—It told of Shiphrah and Puah who "feared God" (Exod 1:21).
—It told of Jael and her bold action:

> She put her hand to the tent peg
>   and her right hand to the workmen's mallet;
> She struck Sisera a blow,
>   she crushed his head;
>   she shattered and pierced his temple. (Judg 5:26)

—It told of Elisha who fed a hundred hungry people (2 Kgs 4:42–44).

In the telling of the faithful, these small stories can be readily continued with contemporary counterpoint, as with actions in present time of generosity and sacrifice amid the virus. The telling of such stories keeps our attention fixed on life-sustaining reality in contexts that seem death-delivering.

2. In seasons of abandonment *people of faith sing defiant songs*. There can hardly be any doubt that singing is an antidote to despair. The songs of Israel are indeed these stories, big and small, set to rhythmic beat. The repertoire of such singing is limited and clearly defined, staying always with the wonderful transformative wonder of God, and with the attentive compassionate mercy of God. The singing constitutes a defiant act that refuses to permit life to be defined by circumstance. Life—the whole life of creation!—rather is occupied by the unutterable wonder of God to which Israel boldly gives utterance. Such singing is unmistakably counter-factual, not unlike the "We Shall Overcome" singing of the Civil Rights Movement. Israel's hope-filled singing is not restrained by the shabbiness of circumstance.

3. In seasons of abandonment *people of faith pray without ceasing*. The prayers of Israel, along with the songs and stories of Israel, focus relentlessly on the wonder of God. The prayers of Israel are prayers of praise and thanks, voicing God as having faithful powerful agency in the world. The prayers of Israel easily address God as "Thou" (You!):

> *Your* way was through the sea,
>> *your* path through the mighty waters;
>> yet *your* footprints were unseen.
> *You* led your people like a flock
>> by the hand of Moses and Aaron. (Ps 77:19–20)

In the presence of this overwhelming "Thou," however, Israel does not hesitate to voice the legitimacy of "I" and "we":

> *I* cry aloud to God,
>> aloud to God, that he may hear *me.*
> In the day of my trouble *I* seek the Lord;
>> . . . *I* think of God, and *I* moan;
>> *I* meditate, and *my* spirit faints. (Ps 77:1–3)

Thus the prayers of Israel, with articulation of "Thou" and claim for "me," gives voice to both sides of the fidelity that sustains in the midst of abandonment.

4. In seasons of abandonment, *people of faith perform story, song, and prayer.* These covenantal acts, however, do not permit faithful people to withdraw into a closed or simplistic sense of "I–Thou" or "me and Jesus." Beyond this rich articulation Israel knows, even in abandonment, that it is a people under mandate, compelled by the commands of Torah. *People of faith practice neighborly obedience.* Thus Zechariah can say, just as Israel emerges from exile:

> Render true judgments, show kindness and mercy to one a another; do not oppress the widow, the orphan, the alien, or the poor, and do not devise evil in your hearts against one another. (Zech 7:9–10)

There is nothing remarkable about this catalogue of obligations, except that it is mouthed just at the cusp of homecoming. In its season of abandonment, Israel had not forgotten—and always remembered—that the performance or covenantal fidelity—even amid abandonment—consists in radical, restorative neighbor actions for those left behind. To the familiar triad of "widow, orphan, immigrant," the prophet adds "the poor." Action toward the left behind who are treasured by God is a primary strategy for resisting despair in abandonment. Equally radical is the warning that Daniel commends even to the exile-causing King of Babylon as an icon of big government. Even big government is summoned to neighborly obedience!

> Atone for your sin with *righteousness,*
> and your iniquities with *mercy to the oppressed* . . .
> (Dan 4:27)

Even abandonment does not diminish the urgency of the life of the neighbor!

These practices that might be given many forms of articulation are disciplines of resistance. Even (or perhaps especially) in dire circumstance of abandonment Israel does not cease to be the faithful people of the absent God. Such actions *refuse despair,* because they constitute an act of both remembering and hoping. At the same time these disciplines *refuse denial* because they look circumstance full in the face. For every praise there is a lament. For every thanks there is voiced need. For every act of neighbor, there is a sense of the legitimacy of self. By such resolved practices faithful people are not overwhelmed by circumstance. They rather redefine circumstance as a venue for a chance to live differently by fidelity that yields energy, courage, and even joy. I am not, dear reader, making this stuff up; you can see it every day among the faithful!

3

Alabaster Cities?

CURRENT UNREST IN OUR cities merits restorative attention. The attention that unrest receives from former President Trump is under the rubric of "carnage" and is anything but restorative. Indeed we can remember that at his inauguration he boldly, and without a cubit of understanding, declared that the "carnage stops now." Of course the unrest has not stopped, and the President has done nothing to stop it (unless we count his "storm troopers"). The reason he cannot stop the unrest is that he has no awareness of or interest in what causes and sustains the unrest. He is unable to grasp the fact that such unrest is inevitable when, over a long period of time, poor and vulnerable people are forced to live in cramped quarters without adequate resources. He is unable or unwilling to connect the dots that by red-lining, zoning, and sustained government resolve such conditions are imposed on a vulnerable population.[1] He does not compute that such policies are the residue of plantation capitalism that thrived on slave labor, and that such policies assure a continuation of thriving on cheap labor from vulnerable people who are kept politically impotent and economically without a future.

1. See Baradan, *The Color of Money*.

We know, already in the Bible, about cities that may fail in injustice. Already in the prophetic tradition we witness a city suffers under *a predatory economy that preys on the vulnerable*:

> Run to and fro through the streets of Jerusalem,
>> look around and take note!
> Search its squares and see
>> if you can find one person who acts justly and seeks the truth . . .
> Then I said, "These are only the poor,
>> they have no sense;
> for they do not know the way of the LORD,
>> the law of their God.
> Let me go to the rich and speak to them;
>> surely they know the way of the LORD,
>> the law of their God."
> But they all alike had broken the yoke,
>> they had burst the bonds. (Jer 5:1, 4–5; see vv. 26–28)

Already there we have a city permeated with injustice that is *sure to be assaulted and destroyed*:

> For thus says the LORD of hosts:
> Cut down her trees;
>> cast up a siege ramp against Jerusalem.
> This is the city that must be punished;
>> there is nothing but oppression within her . . .
>
> And I will make this city a horror, a thing to be hissed at; everyone who passes by it will be horrified and will hiss because of all its disasters . . .
>
> For I have set my face against this city for evil and not for good, says the LORD; it shall be given into the hands of the king of Babylon, and he shall burn it with fire. (Jer 6:6; 19:8; 21:10)

Already in the poetry of Israel we know that such a city will evoke *tears of pathos and loss,* tears by the city and tears for the city as it is remembered and now seen as failed:

> How lonely sits the city
>> that once was full of people!

> How like a widow she has become,
> > she that was great among the nations!
> She that was a princess among the provinces
> > has become a vassal.
> She weeps bitterly in the night,
> > with tears on her cheeks;
> among all her lovers,
> > she has one to comfort her;
> all her friends have dealt treacherously with her,
> > they have become her enemies . . .
> Zion stretches out her hands,
> > but there is no one to comfort her. (Lam 1:1–2, 17)

The city is left helpless and bereft. Already in the horizon of Jesus we see *the city is grieved.* The city is grieved because it "was not willing" to be under the protection of God as a mother hen:

> Jerusalem, Jerusalem, the city that kills the prophets and stones those who are sent to it! How often have I desired to gather your children together as a hen gathers her brood under her wings, and you were not willing. (Luke 13:34)

Already the city is grieved because it *refused to know the things that make for peace:*

> As he came near and saw the city, he wept over it, saying, "If you, even you, had only recognized on this day the things that make for peace! But now they are hidden from your eyes. (Luke 19:41)

The indictment of the city is not credited to the poor who live there. It is credited rather to the leadership-ownership class that insisted on policies and practices of exploitative injustice.

It is easy enough to segue with the rhetoric of loss and grief from that ancient city to our own cities. Failed cities are cities that are ordered in the ways of greed, exploitation, and in our case in racism. Clearly sending in storm-troopers is a foolish gesture that does not even begin to acknowledge the real issues in the wake of oppression of the vulnerable.

I am writing this about cities because of our current urgent unrest and because of the current careless rhetoric of "carnage." (As far as I know the former President Trump has not yet called our cities "shit-holes," though he may have labeled Baltimore, his favorite urban target for his toxic rhetoric, in such a way). I am also, at the same time, thinking about "O beautiful, for spacious skies" that serves as a quasi-pious national anthem for us. Lore has it that Katherine Lee Bates took the train west from Boston, saw the "amber waves of grain" in the Midwest and arrived at the "purple mountain majesty" of Pike's Peak. As her train approached Chicago she saw the impressive sky line of the city that led her to imagine and anticipate a future transformed city "beyond the years." She imagined the city (and other cities; her usage is plural) of "alabaster," "undimmed by human tears." She imagined cities clean, pure, and orderly that had no cause for tears, grief, loss, or pain. She saw beyond present cities that were less than clean, pure, and orderly.

Bates, a college teacher, was alert to justice issues so that her usage of "alabaster" (an odd use at best!) was an innocent image of purity and cleanness. I have wondered, however, if the usage of "alabaster," long after Bates, has come to serve for a distinct future, for "alabaster" is a *white* tinted calcite." Could it be that subsequent singing of the hymn is a dream of pure, clean, well-ordered, *white* city that has purged all the population that contradicts what is clean, pure, orderly, and white? (A saving grace might be that many folk do not know the meaning of "alabaster," or that many folk do not pay much attention to the words as we sing them). I do know that in my erstwhile home town of Cincinnati for decades there has been a sustained effort by zoning and finance to remove Blacks systemically from the city. (Only recently has the city preempted a Black neighborhood for an unneeded soccer stadium!) I have wondered if our uncritical dreaming (and the dreaming of former President Trump) concerns a city *without* poor people, *without* Black people, and *without* poor Black people where "carnage" need not crushed by police action. That racist dream is remote from Bates' poetry and remote from any real social reality. The future of the city that hosts unrest is not a city rid of poor people, or Black people, or poor Black people who are victims of economic injustice and exploitation. That future peaceable city would of course be beyond the ken of the former President Trump and all of those who are recruited by his inflammatory rhetoric.

Of course, there is reason in faith to imagine the coming city that is "beyond the years undimmed by human tears." It is indeed the work of faith to imagine the city promised in the resolve of God. The primary articulation of that coming city—the new Jerusalem—in Isaiah 65:17–25, a new city that will go with a new heaven and anew earth. That new city, however, is not of alabaster. It is a city, rather, constituted by policies and practices of neighborly humaneness—which is of course the only effective way to deal with urban unrest.

—It will be a city *without weeping*, that is "undimmed by human tears":

> No more shall the sound of weeping be heard in it,
>> nor the cry of distress. (65:19)

Why would there be weeping in the city? Well, because of political injustice, because of a weak non-functioning infrastructure, because of a lack of a social safety net for the vulnerable, because of the wealth gap, and because of endless exploitation.

—The coming city will have *no more infant mortality*, because there will be better health care provisions for all:

> No more shall there be in it
>> an infant that lives but a few days,
>> or an old person who does not live out a lifetime;
> for one who dies a hundred years will considered a youth,
>> and one who falls short of a hundred will be considered
>>> accursed. (65:20)

No one dies young!

—The new coming city will be a venue for *secure habitation*:

> They shall build houses and inhabit them;
>> they shall plant vineyards and eat their fruit.
> They shall not build and another inhabit;

they shall not plant and another eat;
for like the day of a tree shall the days of my people be,
   and my chosen shall long enjoy the work of their
   hands. (65:21–22)

Those who build houses and plant vineyards need not be in jeopardy for fear of loss. There will be no exercise of eminent domain whereby the powerful preempt from the vulnerable. There will be no eviction of those who lack adequate resources.[2] The new economy will not be based on the predatory power of the wealthy who greedily covet the property of others:

Alas for those who devise wickedness
   and evil deeds on their beds!
. . .
They covet fields, and seize them;
   houses, and take them away;
they oppress householder and house,
   people and their inheritance.
(Mic 2:1–2; see Isa 5:8–10)

—In the new coming city there will be *no trauma for new-born children*, because all the new born will be protected and cared for:

They shall not labor in vain,
   or bear children for calamity,
for they shall be offspring blessed by the LORD—
   and their descendants as well. (Isa 65:23)

Imagine all the children blessed! With good care and protection, with good pre-schools, and good health care, and none in cages!

The entire economy will be reordered to serve the needs of all of the inhabitants of the city. That of course is the way, the only way to stop urban unrest. The certain way to interrupt so-called "carnage" is with neighborly generosity and intentionality.

And when neighborly generosity is in place, we may trust

—That God will be readily *attentive to the pleas of the people*:

Before they call I will answer,
   while they are yet speaking I will hear. (65:24)

2. See Desmond, *Evicted*.

—That there will be a *reordered life for the environment* without
hurt or danger:

> The wolf and the lamb will feed together,
>> the lion shall eat straw like the ox;
>> but the serpent—its food shall be dust!
> They shall not hurt or destroy
>> on all my holy mountain, says the LORD. (65:25)

The mountains will not be destroyed by strip mining; the rivers
will not be hurt by pollution. The new city imagined in prophetic
vision does not specialize in alabaster. There are no big stately
buildings, but rather a neighborly infrastructure of wellbeing.

Of course we get a reprise on Isaiah 65 in the ultimate biblical
vision of Revelation 21. Yet again new heaven, new earth, and new
Jerusalem (vv. 1–2). The new city is marked in two ways. First, *God
will dwell there*, a riff on Isaiah 65:24:

> See, the home of God is among mortals.
> He will dwell with them;
> they will be his peoples,
> and God himself will be with them. (Rev 21:3)

God had vacated the old Jerusalem (see Ezekiel 10). God has
seemingly abandoned many old cities that are too full of injustice.
In the new city God will be fully present with restorative resolve
Second, there will be *no more tears*:

> he will wipe away every tear from their eyes.
> Death will be no more;
> mourning and crying and pain will be no more,
> for the first things have passed away. (Rev 21:4)

This is a riff on the anticipation of Isaiah 65:19: "No more shall be
heard the sound of weeping." It is, moreover, anticipation of Bates,
"undimmed by human tears." The reason there will be no more
tears is that the ground of tears, loss, and grief will be no more...no
more political oppression, no more predation, no more pollution,
no more poor housing, no more inadequate health care, no more
shabby schools. This is indeed, "All things new" (Rev 21:5)!

The new city that will displace the old failed city is a *gift from God*. It will come "out of heaven from God" (Rev 21:2). But the new city is not only a gift. It is also *a task assigned by God*. As Kamala Harris averred, "We have to do the work." That is why the primary urban theologian in the Bible, Isaiah, can issue a series of urgent imperatives. Isaiah has categorized the old failed city as "like Sodom . . . like Gomorrah" (Isa 1:9), characterized as "like a shelter in a cucumber field" (1:8). But then, after that that sad image of abandonment, the prophet issues a summons:

> Wash yourselves, make yourselves clean;
>> remove the evil of your doings
>> from before my eyes;
> cease to do evil;
>> learn to do good;
> seek justice,
>> rescue the oppressed,
> defend the orphan,
>> plead for the widow. (Isa 1:16–17)

The work of the coming city as *restorative justice* is precisely attentive to the most vulnerable in the community—oppressed, widows, orphans—the ones done in by predation. Isaiah can, after this summons, declare his promissory verdict about what is to come:

> *Afterward* you will be called the city of righteousness,
>> the faithful city.
> Zion will be redeemed by justice,
>> and those in her who repent, by righteousness. (Isa 1:27)

The new city will be a well-ordered community of care, compassion, empathy, and justice. No mention of alabaster; no anticipation of tall edifices like walls or towers (see Isa 2:15). Only neighbors! Neighbors need no storm-troopers. Neighbors do not ponder carnage. To get to the new city, beyond urban unrest, requires us to *receive the generosity of God* and *do the hard work of economic formation* that is committed to the wellbeing of all tribes, peoples, and languages. We may indeed pray that God will "mend thine every flaw" in our present cities!

4

An Alternative Politics

I HAVE HEARD IT reported that nineteen very wealthy families finally control our political economy in the United States; and they do it in covert ways. In Russia that same clique is called "oligarchs." In our society it is called "donors," the ones who use their money to leverage policy. In the Old Testament it is called "the council of the ungodly" (Ps 1:1). They are those who "have no fear of God and no respect for anyone" (Luke 18:4); the Psalms imagine a close linkage between wickedness and excessive wealth. (This phrase in Ps 1:1 is in KJV translation; in the NRSV it is "the advice of the wicked."). The names do not matter so much as the secret reality of a hidden clique that subverts democracy and manages the political economy against the common good.

Full disclosure: I recently reread *Wolf Hall*, the novel by Hilary Mantel on the life and work of Thomas Cromwell, the hatchet man for King Henry VIII. Cromwell, in this rendition, could variously exhibit wisdom, ruthlessness, and sometimes thoughtful mercy. The reason I am writing this brief exposition is that I want to share with the reader two declarations that Mantel places in the mouth of Cromwell. He explains to Henry Percy who, against Henry VIII, defiantly insists that Anne Boleyn is his wife. Cromwell explains to Percy that he is without resources against King Henry:

> The world is not run from where he thinks. Not from his border fortresses, not even from Whitehall. The world is run from Antwerp, from Florence, from places he has never imagined; from Lisbon, from where the ships with sails drift west and are burned up in the sun. Not from castle walls, but from countinghouses, not by the call of the bugle but by the click of the abacus, not by the grate and click of the mechanism of the gun but by the scrape of the pen on the page of the promissory note that pays for the gun and the gunsmith and the powder and shot.[1]

In a second declaration, Cromwell reports to the imperial ambassador, Chapuys:

> The fate of people is made like this, two men in small rooms. Forget the coronations, the conclave of cardinals, the pomp and processions. This is how the world changes: a counter pushed across a table, a pen stroke that alters the force of a phrase, a woman's sigh as she passes and leaves on the air a trail of orange flower or rose water; her hand pulling close the bed curtain, the discreet sigh of flesh against flesh.[2]

These Machiavellian notes faithfully witness to the force of the oligarchs, the donors, and the council of the ungodly. Cromwell is not making a defense of such practice or urging its legitimacy. He is saying what he knows to be the reality of the matter and is prepared to act accordingly. Cromwell is unembarrassed about the matter but believes there is no alternative to this reality.

That leaves us with the wonderment and the yearning that there might be an alternative that lies outside of and beyond Cromwell's sphere of reality that might be effective in generating a different future. The Bible evokes alternative and the deep hope of the human heart breaths otherwise, even beyond the hard realism of Cromwell. Cromwell would have doubted it and not without reason. But our faith is not contained within his realism. In the Bible we may identify two trajectories of faith that evoke another

1. Mantel, *Wolf Hall*, 570.
2. Mantel, *Wolf Hall*, 907.

possibility not contained in the matrix of money and power that Cromwell voiced so clearly and enacted so boldly.

The first such trajectory in the Bible attests a world that is narratively rendered so that *God is featured as the central, lively, and effective agent in the world.* This means that God can be subject of active verbs and can affect God's own purpose of emancipation and restoration in the world. On the one hand this God, unlike any other, is boldly addressed in urgent petition that God would intervene against the wicked who act as if "there is no God" (Ps 10:4; see v. 6). These petitions fully anticipate that God will effectively intervene:

> Rise up, O Lord; O God, lift up our hand;
>> do not forget the oppressed . . .
> Break the arm of the wicked and evildoers;
>> seek out their wickedness until you find none.
>> (Ps 10:12, 15)

> O my help, come quickly to my aid!
> Deliver my soul from the sword,
>> My life from the power of the dog!
>> Save me from the mouth of the lion! (Ps 22:19–21)

> O God, break the teeth in their mouths;
>> tear out the fangs of the young lions, O Lord! (Ps 58:6)

> Rouse yourself, come to my help and see . . .
> Awake to punish all the nations;
>> spare none one of those who treacherously plot evil.
>> (Ps 59:4–5)

On the other hand, the one who petitions affirms that God does hear, answer, and acts, and so gives thanks for divine action:

> From the horns of the wild oxen you have rescued me.
> (Ps 22:21)

> O Lord my God, I cried to you for help,
>> and you have he\aled me.
> O Lord, you brought up my soul from Sheol,
>> restored me to life from among those gone down to the Pit
>>> . . .

> You have turned my mourning into dancing;
>> you have taken off my sackcloth and clothed me with joy.
>>> (Ps 30:2–3, 11)

> I waited patiently for the LORD;
>> he inclined to me and heard my cry.
> He drew me up from the desolate pit,
>> out of the miry bog,
> and set my feet upon a rock,
>> making my steps secure. (Ps 40:1–2)

Such a pattern of rhetoric of course is difficult among us. It is difficult for the "cultured despisers of religion" who long since dismissed such language of divine agency as primitive and obsolete. More than that, it is language that cuts no ice with the oligarchs, the donors, or the members of the council of the ungodly. They long since have settled for autonomy; such language renders the certitudes of the governing clique as penultimate.

Thus it is credible to judge that this rhetoric of divine agency is rhetoric that only works "from below," that is, among those who lack "intellectual sophistication" and who lack as well a kind of connected affluence to make things our way in the world. Thus it is not a question about whether this alternative language is true. Rather the question is "*in what circumstance?*" and "*for whom?*" does this language work. For the powerful such language is foolish; for the excluded and vulnerable such language provides a ground for hope in a world that seems otherwise closed down and without promise.

In his exposition of counter-discourse, Enrique Dussel, following Gramsci, can conclude that the cry of protest from below is "the small door through which Messiah might enter."[3] Dussel judges the practice of such rhetoric in this way:

> The victim who becomes conscious, who erupts with a revolutionary praxis, produces a rupture of "continuous time" [that is, time managed by the covert triad]. He or

---

3. Dussel, *Ethics of Liberation*, 243.

she erupts "remembering" . . . commemorating other
liberatory-messianic moments of past history.[4]

Dussel recognizes that such speech

> Is acceptable today to the ears of a Nicaraguan, of the
> black Africans of South Africa, of the Palestinians in the
> Israeli-occupied territories, or of the *homeless* in New
> Delhi . . . or New York.[5]

This company of protesters of course are belated companions of
the slaves who "cried out" in ancient Egypt and so mobilized the
saving power of God against Pharaoh, and belated companions
of such as Bartimaeus, a blind beggar who refused to be silenced
(Mark 10:48). It is this cry, echoing the long loud cry of ancient Israel, that evokes the emancipatory power of God. This emancipatory power, evoked by loud insistence, subverts the long-standing
certitudes of the oligarchs, the donors, and the members of the
council of the ungodly.

The second such trajectory of alternative historical possibility
we may find in Psalm 1, the very psalm that gives us the phrase,
"the council of the ungodly." That psalm yields a triad of the "cultured despisers of religion, "the wicked, sinners, and scoffers," and
commends and celebrates, to the contrary, *torah-keepers.* The stark
contrast offered in the psalm is between "perish" and "prosper."
Those who perish are the "wicked, sinners, and scoffers," a triad,
not unlike "oligarchs, donors, and the council of the ungodly."
Those who prosper are the torah-keepers. Without putting too fine
a point on it, we may include among the torah-keepers *all those
who "love God and love neighbor" or more simply, those who care for
the neighborhood,* for as Paul avers,

> The whole law (Torah!) is summed up in a single com-
> mandment, "You shall love your neighbor as yourself.
> (Gal 5:14)

---

4. Dussel, *Ethics of Liberation,* 242–43.

5. Dussel, *Ethics of Liberation,* 244.

When we make the category of torah-keepers wide enough, it may acknowledge all those, of whatever ilk, who advocate for social justice and who *put their bodies to the task of protest and advocacy.* These are the ones who generate neighborly prosperity and social wellbeing, the very kind of neighborly prosperity and social wellbeing upon which the covert triad has vigorously defaulted.

Thus we may identify two trajectories of historical possibility that may outflank the oligarchs, donors, and company of the ungodly. As I write this, an affluent couple in an affluent neighborhood in St. Louis is photographed pointing guns at the protesters who occupied their street. The photo, moreover, was circulated by President Trump! The wife of the couple said, "We were frightened for our lives." Indeed when the juices of justice flow in the streets, they do indeed constitute a threat to those who thought they immune to the demanding requirements of the vagaries of history. The march for justice is not deterred by the thick weaponry of the covert triad.

When we ponder these two historical possibilities beyond the covet triad—*the holy power of the transformative God* and *the resilient force of the torah-keepers*—we may wish for a way to link together *the work of God* and *the work of the torah-keeping protesters.* We may find a clue to such a linkage in the ancient "Song of Deborah" that celebrates a victory of the several tribes of Israel over the forces of Canaan. It was a stunning up-set victory against long odds because the Canaanites were formidable in economic and military power. As a result this upset victory was to be gladly celebrated as the song affirms:

> Tell of it, you who ride on white donkeys,
>> you who sit rich carpets,
>> and you who walk by the way.
> To the sound of the musicians at the watering places . . .
>> (Judg 5:10–11)

The victory is to be reiterated and celebrated all the time, as they *ride,* as they *sit,* as they *walk,* as they *gather* at the village wells . . . social places designed for neighborly gossip. (See the parallel of saturation testimony in the Torah practice of Deut 6:7–9.) And then verse 11 identifies the subject of the gossipy celebration:

> There they repeat the triumphs of the LORD,
>   the triumphs of his peasantry in Israel.

In this remarkable poetic parallelism, the "triumph" is said to be "of the LORD" and "of his peasantry." If we take only the first line, the victory is *the singular work of God*. If we take only the second line, the victory is *the spectacular work of the peasants*. If, however, we take both lines together as the poem intends, it is a *both/and*; the holy God and the vulnerable peasants act together in concert. And when they do, the covert triad, in this case the Canaanites, is helpless before them. (Note well that "Canaanites" is not an ethnic designation, but a convenient ideological reference for whoever opposed Israel.)

It is worth rereading the dictums of Cromwell again. He is surely correct in his realism . . . most of the time. Most of the time the powerful in secrecy prevail; but not every time! Sometimes, not often but sometimes, *the ultimacy of God* and *the risk of the vulnerable* converge effectively. And when they do converge, history is turned. That turn may leave "the door ajar, open for Messiah." But even if open less than that, open enough to glimpse an alternative politics, an alternative politics that may generate neighborly justice and a generous economics. It is the task of the preacher to keep before us this alternative that makes the force of the covert triad at best penultimate. It is the task of the church to enter into this alternative account of worldly reality. That is why we accompany the peasants. That is why we sing; that is why we pray; that is why we march!

5

An Unwelcome Read of History

IT IS WELL THAT we keep in mind the fact that not all of American history is recorded. And in some ways we are fortunate that it isn't, for if it were, we might become so chagrined by the discrepancies which exist between our democratic ideals and our social reality that we'd soon lose heart. Perhaps this is why we possess two basic versions of American history: one which is written and as neatly stylized as ancient myth, and the other unwritten and as chaotic and full of contradictions, changes of pace, and surprises as life itself.[1]

We lose so much by our liturgic impatience. We cannot wait, or pause, or sit still long enough. As a result we never to get to say or sing or hear such a marvelous poem as Psalm 105. We get only selected snippets it; it is like memorizing the roster of US presidents, but omitting eight of them "because there are so many of them." The forty-five verses of Psalm 105, with a powerful cumulative effect, is a long recital of the glorious transformative deeds of YHWH that offer a review of the entire sweep of Israel's "canonical" memory. According to this memory, the long journey from Abraham (v. 9) to the land of promise (v. 44) is all accomplished

---

1. Ellison, *Going to the Territory*.

by the compelling power of YHWH, thus a poetic rendition of the Bible from Genesis through the Book of Joshua. In our impatience we miss that grand narrative of God's goodness.

We also miss, at the same time and for the same reason, the long historical recital of Psalm 106 that continues for forty-eight verses. This one we might prefer to miss, because it is a recital of the long-running infidelity of Israel, and Israel's inability and refusal to receive life from the good hand of YHWH. It is a history of sin! The high points of this confessional history of failure include the flowing:

–In response to the miracle of the Exodus, Israel confesses:

> Both we and our ancestors have sinned;
>> we have committed iniquity, and have done wickedly;
> Our ancestors, when they were in Egypt,
>> did consider your wonderful works;
> they did not remember the abundance of your steadfast love,
>> but rebelled against the Most High at the Red Sea.
> (Ps 106:6–7)

This is followed by the pivotal "yet" of YHWH who saved Israel in spite of Israel's rebellious response.

—It is not different in the wilderness sojourn when God provided manna:

> But they soon forgot his works;
>> they did not wait for his counsel.
> But they had a wonton craving in the wilderness,
>> and put God to the test in the desert,
> . . .
> They were jealous of Moses in the camp,
>> and of Aaron, the holy one of the LORD. (106:13–14, 16)

This refusal had a disastrous result, a consequence of rejecting the goodness of God (106:15, 17–18).

—Promptly after the covenant at Sinai, Israel could not tolerate the absence of God, and so had to invent an Ersatz god for itself . . . a calf:

> They made a calf a Horeb
>> and worshiped a cast image.
> They exchanged the glory of God
>> for an image of an ox that eats grass.
> They forgot God, their Savior,
>> who had done great things in Egypt. (106:19–21)

—Even when they entered the land of promise, they did not credit the gift of the land to YHWH, but attached themselves to a Baal:

> Then they despised the pleasant land,
>> having no faith in his promise . . .
> Then they attached themselves to the Baal of Peor,
>> and ate sacrifices to the dead. (106:24, 28)

They entered into transactions with other peoples and so perverted their holy destiny:

> They did not destroy the peoples,
>> as the LORD commanded them,
> but they mingled with the nations,
>> and learned to do as they did.
> They served their idols . . . (106:34–36)

It is no wonder that the Psalm ends with an urgent petition for rescue, apparently from a place of exile:

> Save us, LORD our God,
>> and gather us from among the nations,
> that we may give thanks to your holy name
>> and glory in your praise. (106:47)

This is indeed a sad tale; we in our liturgical impatience are not likely ever to be exposed to it.

When we consider the juxtaposition of Psalms 105 and 106 in the Bible, we can see that 106 follows 105 as something of a "truth squad" and that corrects the uninterrupted celebration of 105. Psalm 106 insists that the "under side" of historical reality must be preserved and presented in the memory and worship of Israel.

What we have then is a *wondrous "canonical" recital* (105) and an *honest corrective* that will not let the doxological wonder of 105 go unchallenged (106). Both psalms are better read (and heard) if taken together. When we read or sing them together, we must endlessly negotiate between the *wonder-telling* and the *truth-telling* that together constitute the treasured narrative memory of Israel that marks it as a peculiar people.

I had this thought about these two psalms when I heard about the "1776 Commission" of former President Trump. In a blatant election maneuver, the president has initiated a study to advance what he calls "citizen education." His notion of citizen education is that it should inculcate our young into the narrative of white male capitalism. Thus Trump proposes to create a US version of Psalm 105 that is filled with uninterrupted celebration of the wonders of white America. His new psalm that would be his core curriculum might affirm:

—That the founders (all slave-owners except for Adams!) were men of immense nobility;

—That the settlement of the new land by white Europeans was an exercise of the "white man's burden," an enactment of the church's ancient "Doctrine of Discovery" that was a warrant for seizure of the new world;

—That US foreign policy is at best noble and at least innocent;

—That US expansionism has been an extension of the rightful superiority of whites and that aggressive trade has brought prosperity to the benighted peoples of the earth.

We might go so far as to imagine that this ode to control might conclude with an echo of the psalm:

> So he brought his people out with joy,
>> his chosen ones with singing.
> He gave them the lands of the nations,
>> and they took possession of the wealth of the peoples.
>> (Ps 105:43–44)

We might even imagine that verse 45, with its "statutes and laws," could be made to refer to the protocols of white superiority that must be kept in place and honored. Such a glorious recital could serve to fend off what Trump calls "leftist anti-American propaganda."

It follows of course that the in president's new curriculum there will be no US version of Psalm 106, no truth-telling that counters the "nice" story written by the winners. This means we may have education:

—That excludes any account of the genocide of Native Americans in an eager confiscation of their lands, a pernicious achievement of Andrew Jackson.

—That denies any recognition of slavery and the 3/5 of personhood for slaves written into the Constitution. At best that "peculiar institution" can be skipped over; at worst it can be mentioned through misleading euphemisms that cover the systemic brutality that is the basis of US wealth.

—That is silent about the Johnson–Reed Act of 1924 that resolutely set restrictive quotas in order to limit immigration from Asia;

—That glosses over the fearful internment of Japanese-Americans during World War II as a threat to white nationalism;

—That denies (or justifies) US practices of torture, most recently in Abu Ghraib but before that water boarding of Filipinos in 1901.[2]

—That refuses to acknowledge (or alternatively to glorify) that the United States is the only nation to have dropped an atomic bomb on civilian populations . . . or anywhere else.

2. Bradley, *The Imperial Cruise*.

The US version of Psalm 106, still to be constructed, (though anticipated by Howard Zinn in his *A People's History of the United States*),[3] is a tale of savage totalism in the service of white privilege and superiority.

Trump, and many others along with him, doesn't want that story known or told. Thus he proposes a rewriting of Psalm 105 as normative and canonical, to the exclusion of any whisper of Psalm 106. This proposed version of the past, moreover, is surely already performed in many so-called "Christian schools" that are to teach our young an innocent version of our past. That version of the past regards any multi-cultural rendering of the past as "leftist anti-American propaganda."

But of course such a false narrative requires great energy and can only be sustained for so long. Even Ronald Reagan, for all of his conservatism, championed an "informed politics," quite contrary to the "deformed" politics proposed and practiced by Trump. Among others it falls to the church to be a truth-teller about US history. Ever since Jesus embodied truth in the face of the Roman governor (John 18:38), it is the DNA of the church to tell the truth. From that, moreover, it follows that the church must also be constructing our own "Psalm 106" about the church's past. That truth-telling narrative would not only bear witness to the Crusades and the Inquisition, but more recent collusions with state-sanctioned brutality. The church must tell its own past so that we may be mindful of the shame-filled ways in which the church (and its leaders) has much too often conformed to the dominant ideology of culture and state.

We may be amazed by and grateful for the fact that Israel's canonical hymnal (the book of Psalms) includes both Psalms 105 and 106. Psalm 105 is important because it attests that the gracious providential role of God has indeed been operative in every part of the history of Israel and by inference in every part of the history of the United States and the history of the church. That affirmation, however, does not negate the need for the truth-telling corrections of Psalm 106 when we are tempted to tell our past only

3. Zinn, *A People's History of the United States.*

"from above." The truth most often arises "from below" which, of course, is why Pilate could not recognize it when it stood before him. We might do our interpretive work on these psalms through the demanding poetry of James Russell Lowell, which he wrote with reference to the Mexican–American War:

> Though the cause of evil prosper,
> yet the truth alone is strong;
> though her portion be the scaffold,
> and upon the throne be wrong;
> yet that scaffold sways the future,
> and behind the dim unknown,
> standeth God within the shadow,
> keeping watch above his own.[4]

FAITH   In the end, the illusions of a false past will be broken by truth-telling. Our society is now at a moment for such truth-telling. That work will not be denied even by the willful cover-up proposed by the president. Patience is required for our liturgical recital in order to hear what Paul Harvey might have called, "The Rest of the Story."

---

4 Lowell, "The Present Crisis," written in 1844 and then published in his volume, *Poems* in 1848. The hymn "Once to Every Man and Nation," was based on the poem.

6

Borders and *Homo migratio*

I GET GOOSE BUMPS whenever I read the words of Isaiah 19:23–25. Those words, in my judgment, constitute the most sweeping radical act of prophetic imagination in the Old Testament:

> On that day there will be a highway from Egypt to Assyria, and the Assyrian will come into Egypt, and the Egyptian into Assyria, and the Egyptians will worship with the Assyrians.
> On that day Israel will be the third with Egypt and Assyria, a blessing in the midst of the earth, whom the LORD of hosts has blessed, saying, "Blessed be Egypt my people, and Assyria the work of my hands, and Israel my heritage."

In order to appreciate the daring intent of this utterance, we need to be aware of the conventional geopolitics of that world in which ancient Israel is set. Israel occupied a land bridge that connected the two superpowers. To the south the superpower was perennially Egypt; to the north the superpower that occupied the territory of the Tigris and Euphrates Rivers changed over time. In the time of Isaiah it was Assyria (contemporary Iraq), and then Babylon, and then still later Persia (contemporary Iran). Over time these superpowers, north and south, sought to control the territory of

Israel as a buffer against the other. Thus the Kingdom of David was perennially under threat and at risk from its neighbors.

In the midst of that risk-producing geopolitics Isaiah uttered this vision of an alternative geopolitics that anticipates "that day" when the rule of YHWH is fully established in the earth. "That day" will make possible a wholly new geopolitics in which there will be free and open passage north and south through Israel from one superpower to the other. There will be free passage and free trade—no borders, no tariffs, no passport control. What makes this new geography possible, declares the prophet, is that in time to come there will not be only people "chosen of God," that is, Israel. What Isaiah has YHWH do is to take three pet names for the chosen people, Israel, and freely assign them to Israel's erstwhile enemies. Thus in time to come Egypt, says God, will be "my people." In the same time to come, Assyria to the north, avers YHWH, will be "the work of my hands." And in that time to come Israel will continue to be, asserts YHWH, "my heritage." All of these are now named as God chosen peoples. The Egyptians can know themselves to be God's "chosen people." Assyrians can as well accept their new identity as God's "chosen people." And of course Israel continues its durable status as God's "chosen people." The only requirement for this status as God's "chosen people" is the recognition that one's neighbors share that status as God's "chosen people." That shared recognition among God's "chosen peoples" makes free passage and free trade possible. By analogue it would be as if the US (that easily claims exceptionalism as God's "chosen people") will recognize Canada and Mexico (and Guatemala and El Salvador) as God's "chosen peoples"! That shared status makes possible the movement of peoples on "the highway" now to be constructed. That day will be, as President Reagan said, time to "tear down that wall."

In the shadow of this remarkable prophetic anticipation I recently read, quite by accident, *The Next Great Migration* by Sonia Shah. Shah has studied the recurrent patterns of movement of human persons and non-human creatures and goes so far as to conclude that migration is essential and indispensible for sustained communal wellbeing. Indeed, she avers: "Linnaeus named our species *Homo sapiens*, Latin for "wise man." A more apt name might have been *Homo migratio*."[1] Shah begins her study with a review of the work of Carl Linnaeus. Linnaeus was a Swede who studied the variety and arrangement of living species, both human and non-human creatures. In 1735 he published his first version of his taxonomy of all species, a taxonomy that became the normative paradigm for much scientific study that was to follow. (He continued to revise and refine his analysis over time.) His work as a bold effort was marked by two features.

First, Linnaeus's taxonomy was static, "unchanging and rigidly ordered" (74). He assumed that the different species had identity and location that were constant, and that species dwelt in and remained in a specific assigned place. Second, his work was marked by a hierarchy of values through which he could easily assert the superiority of some species over others. As this was applied to human species, this static, hierarchal enterprise had a pernicious effect, as it became the taproot of much racism that assigned "good" race to whites and could render value judgments on all races:

> *Homo sapiens europaeus*, the peoples of Europe, were "white, serious, strong," with flowing blond hair and blue eyes. They were "active, very smart, inventive. . .covered by tight clothing. Ruled by laws."
>
> The people who lived in Asia were a separate subspecies called *Homo sapiens asiaticus*. "Yellow, melancholy, greedy . . . Hair black. Eyes dark. Severe, haughty, desirous. Covered by loose garments. Ruled by opinion."
>
> The peoples of the Americas were a subspecies called *Homo sapiens americanus*. "Red, ill-tempered, subjugated . . . Hair black, straight, thick. Nostrils wide; face harsh, beard scanty. Obstinate, contented, free. Paints himself with red lines. Ruled by custom."[2]

1. Shah, *The Next Great Migration*, 216.
2. Shah, *The Next Great Migration*, 87.

One can readily see that the white Europeans became the superior race. After this characterization of "white, yellow, and red," Linnaeus finally could comment on Black people:

> And finally the most distinct subspecies of all was *Homo sapiens afer*, the peoples of Africa. Linnaeus speculated privately that this subspecies might not be fully human but descended from a cross between human and troglodyte. "Black, impassive, lazy . . . Hair kinked. Skin silky. Nose flat. Lips thick. Women with genital flap; breasts large. Crafty, slow, foolish. Anoints himself with grease. Ruled by Caprice."[3]

Shah writes of this taxonomy:

> The most explosive claim in Linnaean taxonomy, that people who lived on different continents were biologically foreign to one another, a claim that would fuel centuries of xenophobia and generations of racial violence, rested on a single bodily part, the sinus pudoris. But very few—quite possibly none—of those who commented on the sinus pudoris had actually ever seen it.[4]

Shah comments that when transatlantic travel became possible people no longer remained in their "assigned" places:

> Most people did not freely mix with people who'd been born on different continents. That would change when transatlantic shipping brought masses of people from Europe, Asia, and Africa together in the New World. People from distinct places would not just glimpse each other from afar or read about each other in stories. They'd brush against each other in alleys, drink at the same bars, and alongside each other on factory floors. They'd fall in love. They'd have babies. Scientists predicted a biological disaster, igniting a social panic that would shape scientific inquiry, law, and politics for decades.[5]

---

3. Shah, *The Next Great Migration*, 87.
4. Shah, *The Next Great Migration*, 89.
5. Shah, *The Next Great Migration*, 92–93.

46   xens - foreign, strange, different

What follows in Shah's exposition is a summary of the consequences of Linnaeus's work and the recognition of Charles Darwin as the one who exploded this static view of the history of species. Darwin's work is to establish that the history of species is a dynamic one open to development wherein change and adaptation are everywhere under way. As a result, there emerged a contest between static and dynamic views of the human species. The articulation of Linnaeus was decisive in funding a racist trajectory of interpretation, in the guise of science, that was powerfully presented by Henry Fairfield Osborn and Madison Grant, New York elites, with a championing of white superiority and supremacy.[6] In 1916, Grant published *The Passing of the Great Race* that "evoked the fear of a hybrid race of people as worthless and futile as the good-for-nothing mongrels of Central America and southeastern Europe."[7] If one listens carefully, one can hear an anticipation of Trump's assessment of "shit holes" around the world.

The great horror of "mixing" led to severe quotas of immigrants in order to keep non-whites out of the United States. The passage of the Johnson–Reed Act (1924) provided strict new quotas that "protected the nation from those who scientists deem racial inferiors."[8] This trajectory from Linnaeus is traced by Shah right up until Paul Ehrlich published his highly influential book, *The Population Bomb* (1971). While his book concerned overpopulation, in fact his concern was rather overpopulation of undesirable non-whites. This concern was also advanced by Garrett Harden in his influential article on the overcrowding of the "commons"; he saw the commons threatened by undesirable populations.[9] While these studies were offered as scientific, the back story of racism is evident, for a population explosion was a threat for the control of white domination and hegemony. As we can see, Shah's exposé is astonishing evidence of the way in which fear pervades even our best scientific research and teaching.

6. See Spiro, *Defending the Master Race.*
7. Shah, *The Next Great Migration*, 111.
8. Shah, *The Next Great Migration*, 125.
9. Harden, "The Tragedy of the Commons."

But Shah also traces out the counter-movement of advocacy from another perspective. The great anthropologist, Franz Boaz, led the way (along with his students, Margaret Mead and Ruth Benedict) beyond a static view of humanity to a much more complex, diverse, and dynamic notion of social reality. It was finally in 1965 under Lyndon Johnson that the Hart–Celler Act was passed "removing race as a criterion for judging whether a migrant could enter the United States."[10] But, of course, the sense of white superiority and the concomitant fear that informed Linnaeus continued to have enormous staying power. Consequently, US immigration policy has been a retreat from Hart–Celler in every way thinkable, until we finally arrive at Stephen Miller and Steve Bannon and "cages" designed to discourage future immigration.

Indeed, we can easily imagine that some in Jerusalem (or Nazareth!) who had heard Isaiah would have strenuously objected. They might have claimed there is only one chosen people (only one!), and the others to the north and south would threaten that status of the "chosen people." Thus the struggle continues in our society that is even now much informed by Linnaeus. It is a struggle that is evident in scripture as well, a struggle that finally depends on the conviction we have about God, God's justice, God's mercy, and God's will for God's creation. Shah's study is part exposé and part advocacy. Finally, she offers a compelling case study for her exposition and concludes that people do move; creatures, including human creatures, do migrate. They migrate for many reasons. Her case-study concerns the wolves on Isle Royale in Michigan. The wolves, isolated on the island, did in-breeding and thereby became weak and degenerate:

> The colony's sole hope: migrants. In 1997 a single wolf made his way to the island. The migrant's jolt of genetic rejuvenation single-handedly transformed the ecosystem. Within a generation the migrant's genes lurked into 56 percent of the wolf population. The number of wolves on the island rose.[11]

10. Shah, *The Next Great Migration*, 163.
11. Shah, *The Next Great Migration*, 260.

Shah concludes: "Nature transgresses borders all the time. And with good reason."[12]

Shah's final chapter is an inventory of the erection of walls around the world. Of these, the ones most familiar to us are the US wall on our southern border and the wall in Israel to fend off Palestinians. Such walls are designed to exclude peoples that are deemed to be a threat (and so unwelcome) to the defining population. Shah concludes that walls finally do not work; they are like a balloon; when pressed in one place, they reappear in another place.

Thus, we have before us the continuing powerful force of the taxonomy of Linnaeus; and we have before us the continuing compelling vision of Isaiah. We can imagine Linnaeus at the border between Israel and Assyria or between Israel and Egypt joining the chant, "Build that wall." At the same time, we can imagine a company of folk around Isaiah who joined to say, "Tear down that wall." It is a contest in which we may participate.

As we do so, we may be aware that in the New Testament the paradigmatic wall (that may be a stand-in for all such walls) is that wall between Jews and Gentiles designed through the Torah to guard, protect, and maintain the singular holiness of chosen Israel (see Lev 19:2). I can think of three texts that evidence the contest over that wall. In Acts 10 Peter, in a trance, is urged by "a voice" to eat unclean food that is prohibited by the Torah (10:13–15). In response to Peter's resistance, the voice declares: "What God has made clean, you must not call profane" (v. 15). From this encounter Peter concluded that: "God shows no partiality" (v. 34) toward clean over unclean, nor to what is holy over what is profane, nor to the chosen over the not chosen. It was this remarkable moment for Peter (alongside the remarkable moment for Paul in Acts 9:1–18) that powered the early church beyond all walls and all distinctions that excluded some and privileged others.

It remained for the writer of the epistle to the Ephesians to provide theological articulation and verification to this awesome moment of tearing down the wall:

12. Shah, *The Next Great Migration*, 251.

> For he is our peace; in his flesh he has made both groups
> into one and has broken down the dividing wall, that is,
> the hostility between us. He has abolished the law with
> its commandments and ordinances, that he might create
> in himself one new humanity in place of the two, thus
> making peace, and might reconcile both groups to God
> in one body, through his cross, thus putting to death that
> hostility through it. (Eph 2:14–16)

What a remarkable moment! How breathtaking! This capacity to
break the wall of chosenness led to the stunning vitality and energy of the missionary church in the early centuries.

We are able to see, moreover, that even Jesus had to learn
to move beyond the border of chosenness. In the demanding
confrontation of Mark 8:24–30, Jesus continued to think that
"the children [Jews] should be fed first." In the narrative a Gentile
woman instructs Jesus beyond his own Jewish horizon: "Sir, even
the dogs under the table eat the children's crumbs" (Mark 7:28).
In a remarkable arrangement of texts, Mark follows that confrontation with a report that Jesus soon thereafter does his second food
"wonder" for the "seven nations," enough to provide "Bread for the
World" that is, enough for all the nations. Seven baskets of surplus
bread are designed for the classic list of seven nations.

It turns out that the breaking of this wall in the New Testament church was a continuation of the great vision of Isaiah of life
beyond borders. This trajectory calls to mind the mantra of which
we are all aware: "What God has joined together let not man [!]
put asunder." God has put all the nations and tribes and tongues
together; ergo, no walls that put asunder. We move in order to
live and to prosper. Such movement is our destiny, boundaries
notwithstanding.

> It is possible to envision a world in which people, too,
> safely move across the landscape. People seeking to move
> as the climate changes or as their livelihoods dry up don't
> have to risk being hunted down by Border Patrol agents
> or drowning in the sea or dying in the desert. Interna-
> tional borders that now bristle with armed guards, razor

wire, and border walls could be made softer and more permeable.[13]

13. Shah, *The Next Great Migration*, 315.

7

Call for Mrs. Thompson!

IN THE TINY TOWN where my dad had his last pastorate, my parents had Mrs. Thompson as their nextdoor neighbor. The one civic contribution that Mrs. Thompson made without fail was to circulate in the neighborhood whenever anyone died in the community. She would knock on every door and ask a dollar contribution from each household. She would put the cash all together and present it to the family of the deceased. She would not have said so, but what she was doing was to help the community grieve the death and signal solidarity with the grieving family. She had this singular skill to abet the grieving process of the community.

Mrs. Thompson would not have known it, but in doing this work she was effectively in the wake of Jeremiah. In his time of crisis, the prophet saw ahead of time that his beloved Jerusalem was on a path to death, destruction, and loss. He could, in his vivid imagination, anticipate the piling up of corpses, too numerous to bury, that we might call by the euphemism, "body bags." They are not "body bags"—they are the bodies of real people who have names, lives, and families:

> for they will bury in Topheth until there is no more
> room. The corpses of this people will be food for the

birds of the air and for the animals of the earth; and no
one will frighten them away. (Jer 7:32b–33)

To further extend his anticipation of the coming death of the city,
Jeremiah issues a call to mobilize the women in society who were,
like Mrs. Thompsons, skilled at grief work:

> Thus says the LORD of hosts:
> Consider, and call for the mourning women [along with Mrs.
>   Thompson] to come;
>   send for the skilled women to come;
> let them quickly raise a dirge over us,
>   so that our eyes may run down with tears,
>   and our eyelids flow with water.
> For a sound of wailing is heard from Zion:
>   "How we are ruined!
>   We are utterly shamed,
> because we have left the land,
> because they have cast down our dwelling." (Jer 9:17–19)

The prophet can line out with specificity the grief that is to
come! He recognized that public grief requires certain skills and
sensibility.

And then he issues an instruction to the skilled women; he
tells them why they must get to their grief work that is most urgent:

> Hear, O women the word of the LORD,
>   and let your ears receive the word of his mouth;
> teach your daughters a dirge,
>   and each to her neighbor a lament.
> "Death has come up into your windows,
>   it has entered your palaces,
> to cut off the children from the streets
>   and the young men from the squares."
> Speak! Thus says the LORD:
> "Human corpses shall fall
>   like dung on the open field,
> like sheaves behind the reaper,
>   and no one shall gather them." (Jer 9:20–22)

He gives the skilled women specific lines that they are to reiterate that voice the great ordeal the loss.

Of course this is, for the prophet, all theater ahead of historical reality. There is as yet no need for the women and not yet a crisis of death. He wants his listeners to anticipate with him and so to change. But his rhetoric is as though the die is already cast and the outcome is certain. Indeed by verse 21 in the lines the women are to speak, he articulates death as a personal agent who forces a way into houses, even into the royal palace with its elaborate security system. No one gets a pass on the consequences of choices made! As with us, no one gets a pass on the force of death!

Since much of our society is in denial (with the rush to re-open) and since we are led by an administration that is wholly incapable of compassion, empathy, or grief, it falls to the church [and its good companions] to do grief work. Such work is to assure that the reality of death is fully acknowledged and that the dead among us are not easily written off and forgotten. That grief work requires skilled folk; the grief should be *long, loud, and public.*

So here is a practical suggestion in order that each victim of the virus should be properly remembered and treasured as more than a passing statistic. Imagine that a big network of churches (a denomination? Presbyterians? Methodists? Lutherans?) assembles a roster of all the dead, parceling out their names, and having all of their names read out in the midst of a congregation in short period of time. It might be in a regular liturgy. It might be in a special community service with appropriate dirge-like music and readings. We may pray that "light perpetual" should shine upon them. In the meantime, however, we may well pause to ponder the loss, to identify with grieving families and communities, and to consider how, in life and in death, we belong to each other and with each other, and for each other in profound ways. We may indeed imagine the dead praying and singing, "Remember me, when you come into your kingdom" (Luke 23:42). Mrs. Thompson and her skilled companions will cause us to pause and remember, because any loss is a loss to us all.

When the church does the work of grieving over our many deaths, it has will have done part of our grief work. I suggest, however, that it is only part of our grief work. Beyond a focus on *our treasured dead*, we have much grieving to do for *a world that is lost* to us beyond recovery. When we engage in deep honesty we know better about our great loss than our eager reopening suggests. We know that the old world of safe American exceptionalism is over. We know that the long-standing advantage of white males is over. We know that the glory days of the institutional church are long gone. We know that there is no going home to the days that were the "good old days" for some of us. We are called now, I suggest, to face the great displacement of our accustomed institutional life. We may from that discernment echo the words that Jeremiah hears on the hearts of his contemporaries, for his words ring true for us now:

> How we are ruined!
> We are utterly shamed . . . (Jer 9:19)

First, there is the honoring of our dead who have not yet been acknowledged or honored. Second there is the deeper relinquishment of our old world. We yearn for an old normal, to recover and "reopen" when the familiar old will be all new for us. Such restoration as real newness, however, requires deep relinquishment for what has failed before we can receive any newness that will let us begin again. Our honest exile precedes our joyous homecoming. It is as Friday must come before Sunday. So our grief must precede any serious newness. When we do that hard work, the church will not be the happiest place in town. But it might be the most honest place in town because the truth of our loss will make us free for the gifts of newness that God will give us.

It is a happenstance of the editorial process that after Jeremiah's dirge in 9:17–23 the next utterance of Jeremiah is an invitation to Israel to choose differently for its future (9:23–24). It is easy to conclude that, not unlike old Jerusalem, we have been "boasting" of the wrong things much too proud of our wisdom, wealth, and might:

the *wisdom of technology,*

the *might of our unrivaled military,*

the *wealth of our consumer economy.*

And now, avers the pot amid the virus, we may choose differently. We may notice that with altered priorities, there are other things about which to boast. We may choose that in which God delights, ready to boast of steadfast love, justice, and righteousness:

steadfast love as *solidarity with the purposes of God,*

justice as *the sharing of resources,* and

righteousness as *investing in communal wellbeing.*

This radical either/or is before us. We will do our choosing not in some big dramatic act, but in the daily grind of policy and practice. The matrix of grief fostered by the skillful women like Mrs. Thompson is an opportunity to think again, to see more clearly and to decide more boldly about the future that will not be a replay of the past. If we yield to the temptation to denial—to deny the great swath of death among us and to deny the loss of our old world—we will choose against the newness of God. Choosing differently is more than Mrs. Thompson would have understood. But she knew enough to get the honesty started. It begins in solidarity that clusters around the loss we all share that we dare not deny. The church is an arena for such honest, generative work of solidarity.

8

Cheap Labor!

COVENANTAL FAITH IN THE Bible refuses all dualisms and holds together matters of *spirituality* and *economics*. It is always a both/and, never an either/or. In the practice of the church, however, an accent on things spiritual has largely muted the accent on economics that is so prominent in the Bible. In more affluent churches, it is predictable that economics will be muted and spirituality made large. In less affluent churches there is a temptation to disregard the heavy burden of economics in the Bible and present instead an extravagant vision of another world to the neglect of this one. Given that recurring tilt that distorts the Bible, it is my estimate that church leadership now must redress this distortion by paying acute attention to economics in the Bible and in our society. For many church leaders this will entail not only close attentive study, but the learning of new interpretive categories and skills as well. Such a redress of energy and attention is not only evoked by our present social circumstance but required by the biblical testimony itself.

When one begins to think about economics in the Bible, one immediately confronts the matter of slavery. After the prologue of the Genesis narratives, the biblical story gets under way in Pharaoh's Egypt. There it is reported that in the midst of acute famine the vulnerable subjects of Pharaoh, in exchange for food, were forced into poverty, loss of land, debt, and finally slavery (Gen 47:13–26). The predatory economy of Pharaoh was based on slavery and required slave labor for the great building projects of the state. Those building included "store house cities" where Pharaoh could store his surplus grain that gave him control over a food-requiring population (see Exod 1:11).[1] Exodus 5 describes the exploitative conduct of slavery in Egypt wherein ever increased "brick quotas" were continually imposed on slave labor (5:10–19). It is entirely plausible to conclude that slavery was not a result of ethnic discrimination, that is, the willful bondage of Blacks because they were Blacks. Rather slavery was instituted because of Pharaoh's need for cheap labor. (The urgency of production was and is quite indifferent to the ethnic identity of cheap labor.) Indeed we may set it down as a truism that where there is *great wealth* (like that of Pharaoh or the later cotton barons) we will find *cheap labor* that makes surplus wealth possible. This is the great starting point for the biblical narrative wherein the emancipatory God intends that the slaves of Pharaoh will be emancipated from their hard labor. The divine mandate that propels the narrative is, "Let my people go" (Exod 5:1).

As a consequence the memory, the pain, and the scar of slavery linger long and deep in the biblical narrative. Israel could, generation after generation, readily remember the abuse and excessively hard demands of the Pharaonic system that aimed at the production of surplus wealth. Israel could recall that the lives of the slaves did not matter; only their work mattered. And when their work was done, their lives were dispensable. The slaves of Pharaoh are indeed "disposable wealth"!

It is remarkable that royal Israel, in its ordering under the Jerusalem elite, could replicate the exploitative practices of Pharaoh. After all, Solomon, the icon of the system, was Pharaoh's son-in-law and seems to have learned from him (1 Kgs 9:24)! The economic shake-down featured in ancient Israel was an arrangement

---

1. See James C. Scott on the political power of stored grain in *Against the Grain*.

whereby *the surplus wealth of the Jerusalem elite* was based on the *subsistence economy of the agricultural peasants* from the surrounding territory whose produce translated into urban wealth. The essential marker of the exploitative system was the practice of cheap labor that made wealth possible. We can identify three notes in Israel's text that continued to echo the Pharonic economy.

The Torah of Deuteronomy offers a social safety-net for the economically vulnerable.[2] Crüsemann comments:

> This whole inner-coordinated system of laws for social security springs from a fundamental Deuteronomic idea: the freedom that has been experienced, which exodus and land represent and which is manifest in the freedom of the agricultural population, includes freedom from payment of tribute or compulsory labor.[3]

Among those provisions Moses commands:

> You shall not withhold the wages of poor and needy neighbors, whether other Israelites or aliens who reside in your land in one of your towns. You shall pay them their wages daily before sunset, because they are poor and their livelihood depends on them; otherwise they might cry out to the LORD against you, and you would incur guilt. (Deut 24:14–15)

The subject of the provision is the "poor and needy" laborers who do the hard work of agriculture. As we know in our own time, there are a host of ways in which vulnerable workers can be cheated out of their wages, not least by withholding payment for a time, a practice that is indeed nothing less than wage theft. These vulnerable workers are surely "cheap labor" whose very lives depend upon daily wages. The Torah provision recognizes that the "livelihood" (*nephesh* = life!) depends on prompt payment. It takes no imagination at all to see that behind this Torah provision is the memory of Exodus emancipation. Indeed, in 24:17, 22 Moses

---

2 See Crüsemann, *The Torah*, 224–34.

3 Crüsemann, *The Torah*, 234.

adds the compelling motivation: "Remember that you were slaves in Egypt and the LORD your God redeemed you from there."

The provision recognizes that to cheat a laborer out of wages is a reiteration of the exploitation of Pharaoh.

The Torah provision is matched in prophetic exposition is the "woe-oracle" that Jeremiah asserts concerning King Jehoiakim (Shallum):

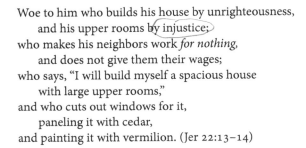

> Woe to him who builds his house by unrighteousness,
>   and his upper rooms by injustice;
> who makes his neighbors work *for nothing,*
>   and does not give them their wages;
> who says, "I will build myself a spacious house
>   with large upper rooms,"
> and who cuts out windows for it,
>   paneling it with cedar,
> and painting it with vermilion. (Jer 22:13–14)

This poem condemns the king's building program for coercing the unpaid labor of his subjects. Beyond the practice of conscription for such labor (see 1 Kgs 5:13–18; 9:20–22), these coerced subjects were reduced to slavery because they worked "for nothing." The poem reflects the royal reality of surplus wealth gotten by cheap labor. The prophet labels such royal policy as violence:

> But your eyes and heart
>   are only on your dishonest gain,
> for shedding innocent blood,
>   and for practicing oppression and *violence.* (Jer 22:17)

It is, moreover, violence that can come to no good end because it is a violence that contradicts the will and purpose of the God of covenant (v. 18). For good reason this royal policy that is sure to fail is contrasted with the father of Jehoiakim, Josiah, whose economic practice was one of justice (v. 15–16). Indeed the poet goes so far as to suggest that good wage policy is equivalent to "knowing YHWH":

> He judged the cause of the poor and needy;
>   then it was well.

Cheap Labor!

Is not this to know me?
says the LORD. (v. 16).

Given this torah provision (Deut 24:14–15) and this prophetic oracle (Jer 22:13–19), it is not surprising, third, that we get a
narrative concerning the economic practice of a king. In Jeremiah
34 it is reported that King Zedekiah (the last king in Jerusalem!),
in a moment of extreme jeopardy, freed those enslaved by royal
policy. Zedekiah made a proclamation, "so that all should set free
their Hebrew slaves, male and female, so that no one should hold
another Judean in slavery" (v. 9). In doing this Zedekiah apparently
enacted the "year of release" authorized in Deuteronomy 15:1–18.
That royal act would be fully congruent with the Exodus provision of Torah and prophet. Then, however, Zedekiah promptly
reversed policy and "brought them again into subjection as slaves"
(Jer 34:11). Clearly Zedekiah's emancipation was an opportunistic
act during an acute emergency; but the king soon returned to stan-
dard royal policy of surplus wealth based on cheap labor. It is for
good reason that the prophet announces a harsh divine verdict on
the perfidious king (vv. 17–22).

When we pay attention to economic matters in the Bible with
an eye on interpretive contemporaneity, it is an easy move from
these ancient descriptions of cheap labor to our own time and
place. It is now beyond doubt that the great modern wealth of the
Western world (and particularly of the United States) is a result of
the cheap labor of slavery. Eric Williams, *Capitalism and Slavery*,
along with many others after him, has traced the way in which the
high demand for cheap labor is what produced slavery,[4] a practice
that Senator Tom Cotton has recently termed a "necessary evil."[5]
Like the brickyards of Pharaoh, the large-scale production of sugar, cotton, and tobacco required cheap labor. Indeed these crops
are endlessly connected to cheap labor in a most exploitative way.[6]
Williams, moreover, is clear that it as the need for cheap labor that

4. Williams, *Capitalism and Slavery*.
5. Lockwood, "Bill by Senator Tom Cotton Targets Slavery Curriculum."
6. See, e.g., Beckert, *Empire of Cotton*.

produced slavery. It was economics, not race that propelled slavery. Race comes only as a belated justification for slavery: "Here, then, is the origin of Negro slavery. The reason was economic, not racial; it had to do not with the color of labor but the cheapness of the labor."[7]

Western wealth, for which the plantation economy is an icon with the provision that white people do not do real work, is based on cheap labor. The lives of that cheap labor, moreover, do not count beyond their capacity to produce. The "slave drivers," were authorized by economic necessity, were to keep the slaves in line and productive (see already Exod 5:10, 15, 19). This is the large truth of the economic wonder of the Western world. Needless to say, the memory, the pain, and the scar of that "wonder" continue among us with compelling force.

The faithful interpreter has in hand both *a biblical sketch of economics* and *an awareness of modern economic history* made simple. With these two bases at hand, biblical and modern, we may critically consider the racial-economic crisis we now face in our society. The immediate evocation of the crisis is police conduct, a culture that has continuity from the old practice of slave drivers to contemporary policing, a continuing mandate to keep blacks in line and productive. But, of course, behind that police culture and resultant conduct is the long-standing assumption that the lives of cheap labor don't matter much. We may notice this already in an early Torah provision: "But if the slave [who has been beaten] survives a day or two, there is no punishment, for the slave is the owner's property" (Exod 21:21). The provision limits the liability of a slave owner for abuse of a slave. And the ground for such limited liability is that the slave is the "silver" (that is, "money") of the owner. The slave owner can do whatever he/she wants, because the slave is property to be disposed of as wanted. Clearly the life of the slave does not matter. It takes no great imagination to go further to say that the lives of the descendants of slaves do not matter either,

7. Williams, *Capitalism and Slavery*, 19; see more recently Baptist, *The Half Has Never Been Told*.

that is, Black Lives don't matter. It is all there in scripture . . . ; a lingering memory, a lingering pain, a lingering scar!

And now appeal is made to other strands of scripture to insist that even slave lives—even the lives of the descendants of slaves, even Black lives—matter. They have mattered since the emancipatory God took the slaves of Pharaoh as the chosen "first-born son" (Exod 4:22). Of course, such an affirmation requires a move from *Israelites as slaves* to *Blacks as slaves*, or *other oppressed peoples as slaves* who are made in the image of God and who have first-class membership within the rule of the creator God.

It is the hard work of biblical interpretation to do the teaching that subverts what had become "normal" in ancient Israel and what has become "normal" in the modern world. It is "normal" to think that cheap labor is expendable, subject to whatever abuse, oppression, or disregard that might be required by the ownership class in its commitment to surplus wealth through cheap labor. The biblical interpreter has on hand the new "normal" that disrupts the old calculus of surplus wealth and cheap labor. The old norms have been sustained by habit and by law that have assumed that Black members of society are *substandard persons* destined for *sub-standard schools*, *substandard housing*, and *substandard menial jobs*. This "normal" is so well established among us that we do not even notice it even when we observe it every day. And now we face the undoing of that insidious "normal." That undoing cannot be accomplished without economic revision of a most serious kind. It cannot be undone without the deep expose of habit and law and the way we have read scripture. The good news of the Bible, the economic good news of the Bible concerns the undoing of our "normal" that has for too long specialized in privilege and advantage of acute kind.

The start of the undoing is to filter our economic passion and interest through the lens of biblical testimony. It cannot accidental that Jesus told a parable about generous pay (Matt 20:1–18). Of course, the parable is about more than economics. But it is about economics! It is about generous pay for workers who are treated with high regard. The parable, at its finish, is about "the last becoming first." In much of the Bible, in Western history, and now among us the "last" have been last for a very long time. Now, just now, we have to think again that the last will not be and cannot remain last among us. A start on this emancipatory prospect is to end cheap pay and relinquish some surplus wealth. This new normal is a lesson about the inversion of last and first. It is a lesson always learned again, from Pharaoh forward.

9

Clued to the Big Moment

IT IS NOT EASY now to let Christmas be a singular moment of faith and life. On the one hand, commercialism—even before Thanksgiving—detracts from the moment of birthed newness. On the other hand, the demands of Covid-19 make every day seem like the next one and the last one, and we don't easily recognize "why this day is different from all other days." On both counts, the church's attentive focus on the decisive moment of Christmas is a summons that requires some energy. In the epistle reading for the day, Paul invites the congregation to order its life so that it may "be kept sound" (undamaged, undiminished) for the *parousia* of our Lord Jesus Christ. Paul has no doubt that ordinary time will be deeply disrupted and we do not want to miss out on that disruption. Our season of overblown commercialism will be disrupted; the despairing sameness of the virus will be disrupted. In his early pastoral guidance in 1 Thess 5:16–24, Paul issues three imperatives to the faithful for their readiness. In the verses just prior to this, we find:

- respect pastoral leaders and esteem them (vv. 12–13);
- be at peace among yourselves (v. 13);

- be patient (v. 14); and
- seek to do good . . . to all (v. 15). *Do not quench the Spirit*

Nothing here about gift-giving, or shopping, or decorations, or sending cards, or pageants! Just neighborliness that enhances human dignity and wellbeing! That is, for Paul, the requirement for Christmas preparation (for the Parousia!), for the moment of his coming. Paul anticipates that those in his pastoral charge should put some energy into preparation. That is, of course, a very different energy from the kind that leaves many of us mostly exhausted by Christmas day. Paul writes to the congregation at Thessalonica on the assumption that his readers are knowledgeable about faith and are clued in for the time. I can identify three facets of this assumption on Paul's part.

First, Paul expects his readers in the church to *know what to do*. He issues three expectations to them, each of which is surely counter-cultural:

1. *Always rejoice*! Joy is a core theme for Paul, but it is not to be confused with our commercialized exuberance at Christmas. Nor is it "Christmas joy" that comes in a bottle. Rather Christmas joy, for Christians, is a deep, glad confidence that God's good will for the world will outrun all of our troubles and tribulations. This is not a Pollyanna denial; Paul is able and willing to look trouble squarely in the face. But he always regards the troubles of the world as penultimate, because beyond such vexations are the capacity and readiness of God to work a newness that is not a reshuffle of what is old. Thus Christmas joy is based in the long game of God's rule over all evil, including the ultimate evil of death. For that reason Christmas joy has Easter on its horizon. This is the same Paul who later on will write: "Nothing can separate us from the love of God. . . not even death" (Rom 8:38–39)!

2. *Always pray* . . . without stopping! For Paul prayer is neither an occasional pious act nor an exercise in "thoughts and prayers." It is, rather, an act whereby the world is held up to God in all its neediness in the confidence that the God addressed in our prayers has the capacity for a transformative response. The reason for not

"ceasing to pray" is that the world and all of its creatures are penultimate and are finally dependent upon the good gifts of the creator God for life and for wellbeing. Thus constant prayer is a way in which our lives are regularly and confidently addressed back to the God who gives life.

3. *Always give thanks!* "Thanks" is a ready acknowledgment that we are on the receiving end of life from the God who gives more than we can ask or imagine. Thanks is the creaturely counterpart to God's incessant and bottomless generosity. It is the ready affirmation that we do not possess anything that is not a gift to us (see 1 Cor 4:7). Thanks is a glad acknowledgement that we live by unmerited grace, by undeserved generosity, by inexplicable gift. Thanks is not a calculating bookkeeping enterprise, but an overflow of awed recognition that we are the beneficiaries of God's life-assuring gifts.

It is worth considering these three acts in light of our conventional Christmas practice:

- This is an invitation to *joy* that may discipline Christmas *fatigue*;

- This is an invitation to *pray* that is an antidote to our *busyness*;

- This is an invitation to *thank* that may counter our *excessive programmed management of our resources*.

We know what to do!

Second, Paul invites his readers to know *what to receive*. Everybody, not just children, look forward to getting gifts at Christmas. It is very nice to be on the receiving end of gifts. It is also a vexation sometimes to know what to give. Paul counters all of that with an awareness that what is being given to us by the creator God is "the Spirit" (v. 19). For starters, the Spirit is the breath of life that we, moment by moment, inhale as a free gift, even in the midst of the deepest smog and pollution. The spirit is the surge of vitality from the creator God that we cannot muster for ourselves, so that we are not and cannot be and need not be self-starters. In context, the Spirit is the surge of courage that may come upon Christian congregations in their worship and obedience, a force from God that tilts toward newness and that is effectively transformative in the life of the congregation.

Evidence of the work of the Spirit was, among other things, found in the presence of prophets who spoke outside all conventionality, inviting new thought, new vision, and new possibility. Evidently there were those who resisted such surges of newness as too unsettling and too demanding. In response to such resistance, Paul issues two pastoral imperatives. First, do not *quench!* Do not try to stifle the gift of newness that comes from the wind of God, but be open to that newness. Second, *test* such surges of newness to make sure that they cohere with the primary claims of the gospel. The image that emerges in Thessalonica is a Christian congregation that is not worn and haggard by "Christmas preparation," but that is in a receptive posture for newness that is the gift of God. Such a newness of course shakes and shatters our old comfort zones, but that is how it is with God's transformative capacity. Members of this congregation likely were not into shopping for Christmas gifts. They could, however, be discerning where the gift of God's newness was intruding into their lives in ways that both transformed and challenged.

Third, Paul invites his readers to *know what time it is*. In our commercialism of Christmas we notice that in most shopping venues there is no clock. Commercialism wants to banish time, make all time timeless in self-forgetting indulgence. To the contrary, Christians know what time it is. It is time for the *parousia*, the coming of our Lord Jesus Christ. Paul readily utilizes the rhetoric of apocalyptic in order to witness to the coming of Jesus. That rhetoric, however, is drawn close to the dailyness of lived reality when we consider how Jesus "came" in the "coming of our Lord Jesus Christ" (v. 23). The "coming" we celebrate is in the dramatic scene of Bethlehem with the wondrous cast of angels and shepherds, and Caesar lingering much too close at hand. But of course Paul does not seem to know the tale from Bethlehem. What he knows, rather, is the myriad of stories that circulated in the early church that variously were about a leper healed, a blind man seeing, a lame man walking, a dead man raised to new life. . .one at a time. The true "apocalyptic" of the earliest memory concerns transformed lives that constituted the routing of the kingdom of evil and death in specific, quite concrete cases.

Very much of our commercialized Christmas observance, reiterated by the busy preoccupation of the church, has lost sight of the dangerous and transformative power that defines "the coming." The familiar beauty of the Christmas pageant no doubt has its place. But the true "coming" that is to be celebrated is the astonishing capacity of God to restore to life the lost dimensions of our creaturely capacity. We now live in a world where the kingdom of death is surging—in the virus, in the failed economy that breeds starvation for many, in our ready embrace of brutality, and in the surge of anti-neighborly, fearful greed. This is the truth that is right in front of us. It is not, however, the whole truth. It is not the truth entrusted to us. The truth entrusted to us is that there is a "coming one" who in actual bodily ways rescues from the power of death.

That, of course, is our cause for celebration. In order to celebrate well we must know,

- *What to do*: rejoice, pray, thank;
- *What to receive*: the spirit;
- *What time it is*; it is the very edge of the coming.

The diminishment of Christmas among us or its distortion in too busy fatigue is obvious to all of us. This means that in our more-or-less post-Christian culture, I suppose, that there are many folk, inside the church as well as outside the church, who have little notion about the invitation or the summons of Christmas. Thus it is the pastoral task of the church to teach ways to keep Christmas faithfully. This is not to harp against commercialism because that is too easy. And anyway, that train has left the station. Our accent is not on what *not* to do, but on *what* to do. We will only do what we know. And because of this paragraph from Paul we know a great deal:

We know what to do;

We know what to receive;

We know what time it is.

Paul finishes this paragraph with a mighty assurance: "The one who calls you is faithful, and he will do this! (v. 24).

God calls us to this moment of in-breaking. God is faithful. God will do "this," that is, God will bring newness in the coming of our Lord Jesus Christ. Our work is to watch for the in-breaking of that newness. That newness happens here and there, now and then when the frontiers of evil and death are pushed back, when the advances of deathliness are repelled. Our Christmas celebration will be most rich and wondrous when we are kept "sound and blameless" (1 Thess 5:23).

10

Destiny, not Fate

ONE OF OUR TRUMP-INCLINED neighbors who will not wear a mask says, "Well, if I die it must be my time." Our roads, moreover, are strewn with signs that say, "God's got this." These judgments, if taken seriously, conclude to that we are fated to a future that is already determined for us. This sentiment is an echo of the ancient confidence in the "law of the Medes and the Persians." Thus the lesser authorities in Persia say to King Darius,

> Now, O King, establish the interdict and sign the docu-
> ment, so that it cannot be changed, according to the law
> of the Medes and the Persians, which cannot be revoked.
> (Dan 6:8, 12, 15)

This sentiment, ancient and contemporary, is a wish for and confidence in a world that is settled, secure, stable, does not change, and cannot change.

This sense of fate, when uttered, seems to locate life in a deep trust in God "whose got the whole world in his hands. In fact, however, it is statement of despair and resignation, without hope or expectation for anything new. The signs along the road and the statement of my neighbor together bespeak a sense of helplessness before circumstances that are beyond our control. It amounts to a *loss of agency*, when being an agent is understood as the capacity to act in order to open new futures for self, for neighbor, and for the world. When one loses agency, one is a passive recipient of what comes, whether what comes is from God or from elsewhere. It is a refusal to take any initiative or responsibility beyond the present *status quo.*

When I think of about "loss of agency" I am drawn to Psalm 115. In that Psalm, it is readily affirmed:

> Our God is in the heavens;
>> he does whatever he pleases. (v. 3)

Witness to YHWH as effective agent requires only this terse affirmation. By contrast the Psalm lingers with in a detailed characterization of idols that are quite unlike YHWH:

> Their idols are of silver and gold,
>> the work of human hands.
> They have mouths, but cannot speak;
>> eyes, but do not see.
> They have ears but do not hear;
>> noses, but do not smell.
> They have hands, but do not feel;
>> feet, but do not walk;
> they make no sound in their throats. (vv. 4–7)

The sum of these markings is that the idols re inanimate and powerless; they can do nothing. Indeed the "sound they cannot make in their throats" is "ahem." They cannot clear their throats! But the point to notice is the derivative statement of verse 8:

> Those who make them are like them;
>> so are all who trust in them.

Those who worship and trust in powerless idols become like the idols they worship, powerless and inanimate. The idols have no agency; those who worship them come as well to have no agency. I do not conclude that my neighbor is a worshipper of idols. But I do conclude that she has willingly signed on for a world in which she is neither permitted nor expected to exercise agency. She understands herself to have no role to play in the shaping of the future that is to come upon us. I fear, moreover, that the Church's singular insistence upon grace from God has become "cheap" in the sense that it seems not to consist in a call to or offer of agency. In the Psalm we have:

—the negative: worships idols . . . become like idols;
—the positive: worship the God who freely does what he pleases . . . (implied) become free like the God of freedom.

The covenantal-prophetic tradition of the Old Testament to which Jesus is an heir is an invitation to agency as a part of the human role in covenant. One can see in the symmetrical statement of Deuteronomy 26:17–19 the assumption that YHWH's covenant partner has an active role to play in the life of the world. On the one hand YHWH has agreed "to be your God" (v. 17). On the other hand, Israel has agreed to be YHWH's "treasured people" (v. 18). The role of this treasured people, in the horizon of Deuteronomy, however, is not a one-dimensional, blind, unthinking obedience. As the book of Deuteronomy makes clear, being responsive to YHWH' "statues, commandments, and ordinances" requires active interpretive engagement and decision-making about the concrete shape of fidelity. Thus the covenantal tradition of Deuteronomy posits Israel as a community at work in order to generate an alternative future. Indeed, if one considers the commandments concerning socio-economic justice, it is clear that responsible obedience is subversive of the *status quo*, for it concerns debt cancellation (Deut 15:1–18), loans without interest (23:19–20), prompt payment of workers (resisting wage theft) (24:14–15), and a generous safety net for the disadvantaged (24:17–22). This is no ordinary preoccupation with "religion." Rather it is the enactment of an alternative social reality. Thus, the big imperative in Deuteronomy is "choose": "*Choose* life so that you may live" (Deut 30:19). Israel has alternatives from YHWH that require agency. It can choose the idols of the status quo impotence, or it can choose a covenant life I sync with the creator God.

Deut 30:11-20

And, of course, it is not different in the prophetic tradition. The prophets characteristically declare that disregard of covenantal stipulations can only bring big trouble. The recurring prophetic indictment is that Israel has refused to enact the agency in performing an alternative world. The prophets regularly conclude that the failure to perform that agency can only bring disaster, even upon the "chosen" people. For good reason, the prophets summon Israel to return to covenant and to enact of covenantal agency:

> Wash yourselves; make yourselves clean;
>> remove the evils of your doings
>> from before my eyes;
> cease to do evil;
>> learn to do good;
> seek justice,
>> rescue the oppressed,
> defend the orphan,
>> plead for the widow. (Isa 1:16–17)

> If you return, O Israel, says the LORD,
>> if you return to me . . .
> and if you swear, "As the LORD lives!"
>> in truth, in justice, and in righteousness,
> then nations shall be blessed by him,
>> and by him they shall boast. (Jer 4:1–2)

> If he does not eat on the mountains
>> or lift up his eyes to the idols of the house of Israel,
> does not defile his neighbor's wife
>> or approach a woman during her menstrual period,
> does not oppress anyone
>> but restores to the debtor his pledge,
> commits no robbery,
>> gives his bread to the hungry
> and clothes the naked with a garment,
>> does not take advance or accrued interest,
> withholds his hand from iniquity,
>> executes true justice
> . . . he shall surely live. (Ezek 18:6–9)

> But let justice roll down like waters,
>> and righteousness like an ever-flowing stream. (Amos 5:24)

These are all calls for agency!

It is not, of course, different with Jesus who is situated in the covenantal-prophetic stream of Israel. He sent his disciples out with a mandate:

> Cure the sick,
>   raise the dead,
> cleanse the lepers,
>   cast out demons. (Matt 10:8)

> Cure the sick who are there, and say to them, "The kingdom of God has come near to you." (Luke 10:9)

This set of imperatives closely echoes Jesus own performance, as in Luke 7:22. This set of imperatives intends that his disciples should open new futures for those whose present circumstance is skewed toward despair. Clearly the disciples are empowered and expected to exercise agency in generating new social possibilities.

As I was thinking about agency toward newness, I read Mary Doria Russell's book, *A Thread of Grace: A Novel*.[1] Her book is a remembrance of the way in which generous Italians of every stripe protected Jews in the midst of the Holocaust. Russell has an elder, Iacopo, deliver this reflective affirmation:

> The sages offer us a way to understand the terrible times when we are driven into exile, when we are beaten and enslaved, when we are killed with less thought than that a *shochet* gives chicken. The Holy One has made us His partners, the sages teach. He gives us wheat, we make bread. He gives us grapes, we make wine. He gives us the world. We make of it what we will—all of us together. When the preponderance of human beings choose to act with justice and generosity and kindness, then learning and love and decency prevail. When the preponderance of human beings choose power, greed, and indifference to suffering, the world is filled with war, poverty, and cruelty. Bombs do not drop from God's hand. Triggers are not pulled by God's finger. Each of us chooses, one by one, and God's eye does not turn from those who

---

1. Russell, *A Thread of Grace*.

suffer or from those who inflict suffering. Our choices are weighed. And, thus, the nations judged.[2]

The accent of this statement is on the human capacity to choose a better future, one of risk and of generativity. The either/or of the elder, Iacopo is clear enough: *a concern to guide the next generation*

      —either: justice, generosity, kindness,

      —or: power, greed, indifference to suffering.

Each choice will inescapably yield futures

That sense of agency is compellingly reflected in verses in the Song of Deborah in Judges 5. In the song Israel celebrates a great victory over the Canaanites. It reports that at the village wells ("watering places") the victory is told and retold:

> There they repeat *the triumphs of the* LORD,
>   the *triumphs of his peasantry in Israel.* (5:11)

What interests us is the poetic parallelism that characterizes the triumph:

      —the triumph is fully a work of YHWH (to God be the glory!)

      —the triumph is the work of Israel's peasants.

The song affirms that both are indispensable. No victory without the agency of YHWH. But also, no victory without the agency of the peasants. It is a both/and, not an either/or. Israel characteristically understands that futures are created by human agency, the agency to which God's people are summoned in both the law and the prophets.

We may wonder, then, why my neighbor refuses the manifest future-creating chance of mask wearing and why the one who posts the road signs chooses to eschew human agency. Well, for one thing, it is easier! It avoids all risk, all venture into an ill-defined possibility. That choice (no doubt made unwittingly) is a decision for a changeless *status quo* world in which no real future

---

2 Russell, *A Thread of Grace*, 158–59.

is expected or thought to be possible. The refusal of agency is to opt for an abiding present tense of impotence and helplessness. And, of course, that option is variously encouraged by powers that prefer that we should rest in impotence. It is of course the case that "cheap grace" declared by the church can be a bid for abdication and resignation.

If, however, we are those who worship the God who "does whatever he pleases" (Ps 115:3), we are in the image of that God and not in the image of any impotent idol. That reality calls us to be exercise freedom for the sake of newness according to the intent of the God whose image we perform. I suggest, then, that it is the work of the church and its ministry to invite, summon, and empower members of the body of Christ to embrace agency in generating alternative futures. It is not obvious how that work of invitation, summons, and empowerment is to be done. But surely it has to do with the recognition that God's world is not fixed and closed, but is a creation underway toward newness. The recovery of the theme of creation as an open-ended process is crucial. In that context, effective human agents,

—are *deeply rooted in memories* that attest, remember, and treasure old performance of agency, both divine and human;

—are *transformatively located in a world that is under promise*, so that faith is indeed the work of seeking "a new country" that is our true "homeland" (Heb 11:14–16). That "homeland" is not about life after death, but concerns the coming of God's new creation so that God's will is done "on earth as it is in heaven."

—are *skilled in doing social analysis* that effectively connects the dots of money and power.

In the covenantal-prophetic-apostolic tradition, ministry is the process of permitting members of the body accept agency for themselves and for their neighbors. In that world there is no cause—and no excuse!—for abdication or resignation. In the world of the gospel we are not fated like "Medes and Persians." We are rather, as the beloved of God, destined toward wellbeing. We need only choose that wellbeing in active, daring, wise ways. That is how we may live and prosper in our present "land of promise" (see Deut 30:20).

11

Discipleship That Inconveniences

COMPLETE UNWAVERING DISCIPLESHIP TO Jesus is costly, eventually leading to a risky contradiction with dominant culture. Most of us, surely, are not much inclined to that costliness that seems nothing short of heroic. Most of us will settle for a lesser discipleship. Even that lesser discipleship, however, inconveniences. Here I reflect on that inconvenience because one of the great gifts of contemporary consumer culture is that everything is made convenient for those who have money for access.

> Convenience is the major selling point for technology. Our technology-supported lives have now become so convenient that we experience the practices of neighborliness as being greatly inconvenient. Walking. Handwriting. Borrowing sugar. Convenience is what the market sells. It is a surcharge added to the cost of community. The market's promised convenience and speed turn out to have a hidden cost . . . Speed and convenience don't build neighborliness.[1]

At the very least, the call of Jesus is to inconvenience.

1. Block, Brueggemann, and McKnight, *An Other Kingdom*, 26.

I could think of two texts that concern a call to inconvenience. In Joshua 24 Joshua asserts that he and his household are committed to covenantal obedience to YHWH: "As for me and my household, we will serve the Lord" (v. 15) He also invites his listeners to choose for the God of the covenant:

> Now if you are unwilling to serve the Lord, choose this day whom you will serve, whether the gods your ancestors served in the region beyond the River or the gods of the Amorites in whose land you are living. (Josh 24:15)

In response the assembly answers Joshua by reciting the narrative "credo" of past history with YHWH (vv. 16–18), and concludes: "Therefore we will serve the Lord, for he is our God" (v. 18). That ready response, however, strikes Joshua as too facile. So he warns the community:

> You cannot serve the Lord, for he is a holy God. He is a jealous God; he will not forgive your transgressions or your sins. If you forsake the Lord and serve foreign gods, then he will turn and do you harm, and consume you, after having done you good. (vv. 19–20)

A second time the community indicates its readiness for covenant:

> No, we will serve the Lord (v. 21)!

Joshua then warns of the high risk of their decision for YHWH:

> You are witnesses against yourselves that you have chosen the Lord to serve him (v. 22).

They answer yet again:

> We are witnesses.

Joshua then insists that they put away foreign gods; they answer one more time:

> The Lord our God we will serve, and him we will obey (v. 24).

Then and only then does Joshua make covenant:

So Joshua made a covenant with the people that day, and
made statutes and ordinances for them at Shechem. (v. 25)

The "statutes and ordinances" are surely an inconvenience for
those who embrace the covenant. This is a curious give-and-take
that must have exasperated the community. But Joshua is insistent. Entering into covenant with YHWH is no easy or light thing
and must not be entered easily or lightly. Joshua's insistence shows
the risk and demand of this faith, and seeks to make clear that
covenant with YHWH is inconvenient and a serious disruption of
business as usual. What follows in the Book of Judges makes clear
that they had not understood how inconvenient faith in YHWH is,
for they persistently "went after other gods." We might well offer a
riff on the "gods of our ancestors" that can no longer be practiced
because this covenant is mutually exclusive! Those "gods of our
ancestors" might include racism and nationalism and the entire inventory of oppressions now so familiar to us. That they are "gods"
is indicated by the fact that they have been taken among us for
so long as absolute and beyond question, so much endorsed and
affirmed by so much of the church!

A second text to consider is the narrative of Jesus with his
disciples in Mark 10:35–45. It is clear that at this point in Mark's
gospel that the disciples had not understood Jesus' teaching or
mission. They "innocently" request places of privilege in his coming kingdom of glory (v. 37). They imagined that in Christ's new
rule they would, as his faithful followers, be ascendant in power
and honor, all so convenient as a pay-out for discipleship. Jesus,
however, contradicts this fairy tale of convenience. He reminds
them of the "baptism" and the "cup." The baptism is recruitment
into the new regime that will frontally contradict the ways of all
old regimes. Indeed this baptism is not unlike Joshua's "put away
foreign gods." The "cup" that must be drunk is the destiny that
in the case of Jesus led to his execution at the hands of the state
(Mark 14:37). The disciples had understood neither baptism nor
cup, both of which concern obedient suffering. They still do not,
for they much too readily answer, "We are able" (Mark 10:39).
They still imagined privilege in the coming regime, recognizing

nothing of the disruption, risk, or cost. But of course in their lack of understanding, they grossly misjudged. Jesus had to tell them that all he had to offer was a baptism and a cup, not any privileged seating in time to come:

> The cup that I drink you will drink; and with the baptism
> with which I am baptized, you will be baptized; but to sit
> at my right hand or my left is not mine to grant, but it is
> for those for whom it has been prepared. (v. 40)

The baptism and the cup are much more than an inconvenience. But they are, at the outset, at least that. It is from this text that Bonhoeffer could declare, "He bids us come die with him."

The two narratives of Joshua and Jesus make clear that embrace of this faith as a living practice cannot go along with business as usual. For Joshua, it means abandonment of "foreign gods," loyalties inimical to covenant. For Jesus it entails practical contradiction to the dominant culture. That contradiction led him to the conclusion that greatness is textured as servanthood." Both narratives concern convenience interrupted.

I have thought of two instances of such an interruption of convenience. First, a friend of mine had ordered a book from Amazon. I gently reprimanded her for colluding with Amazon, that great mocker of democracy that depends on cheap labor and that is about the work of destroying local economies everywhere. Her response was, "But it is so convenient." Of course it is! It intends to be. It intends to outflank local shopping with convenience and so to remove money from the local economy toward those who have no interest in or investment in local society. Local shopping is inconvenient, something like handwriting and borrowing sugar mentioned above. I suggest then that local shopping (with its extra costs) and refusal of on-line convenience is a modest act of discipleship, a readiness to be inconvenienced for the sake of the neighborhood.

Second, I can think of nothing more inconvenient than the practice of sabbath. If and when we keep sabbath seriously and faithfully, it exacts the foregoing of many favorite activities we like and prefer to do. But sabbath is meant to be inconvenient. It is meant to interrupt our favorite activities and now surely our favorite electronic connections. It means to interrupt our initiative-taking actions in order that we might for an instant be, without distraction, on the receiving end of the generosity of God.

It is likely that the social economy of the well-off will become, with technological advances we can scarcely anticipate, more and more convenient for us. But such ever-advancing convenience is like a screen that causes us not to notice the world around us. With convenience as a narcotic, we do not notice those who are, by policy as well as by practice, not included in our orbit of convenience. We do not notice the cheap labor of those upon whom our convenience depends. This it occurs to me that we might focus more closely on the ways in which our convenience undermines our neighborliness and thus detracts from our capacity for obedience to the Gospel. The path of some inconvenience just might be a way of inviting us away from the gods that would make us ourselves the center of the universe. It might be a way to embrace the baptism that inducts us into an alternative world. The path of inconvenience just might be a first sip of the cup of discipleship that we may drink as participants in the new regime. It is clear, is it not, that the gods of convenience do not care for mercy, justice, righteousness, or neighborliness, that is, do not care for the realities of covenantal life. Inconvenience is not radical discipleship and it must not be confused with that. It might, however, be a way whereby we become a bit more "woke" about our life of faith.

12

Do the Numbers!

MEET AMOS WILDER (1895–1993). Wilder was a pastor, a poet, and a long-time New Testament scholar at Harvard. He was also the brother of Thornton Wilder, author of *Our Town*. I introduce him to you, dear reader, in order that you may, along with me, savor his wonderful enigmatic dictum: "The zero hour breeds new algebra." Every element in this sentence evokes careful attentiveness as each element is thick with intent.

The zero hour is the moment when we reach the nadir of possibility and have no reason to anticipate any good prospect. The zero hour is devoid of capacity and brings us into the depth of despair. In ancient Israel the zero hour was the exile of defeat, destruction, and displacement when the holy city and its temple were destroyed and God's promises had run out. Israel had no possible future:

> My way is hidden from the LORD,
>   and my right is disregarded by my God. (Isa 40:27)

> But Zion has said, "The LORD has forsaken me,
>   My Lord has forgotten me." (Isa 49:14)

> They say, "Our bones are dried up, and our hope is lost;
>   we are cut off completely. (Ezek 37:11)

Do the Numbers!

That moment of despairing resignation is reiterated in the New Testament narrative in the execution of Jesus. In the wake of that Friday, the disciples could assert: "But we had hoped that he was the one to redeem Israel" (Luke 24:21). The verb "hope" is in the past tense. Now hope is gone. That same moment of hopelessness arises for us personally and publicly when our lives are broken beyond repair. Just now, of course, amid economic meltdown and the virus we are, in our society, at something of a zero hour. Our leaders continue to assure, "We will get through this," or "We will get through this together." But there is for now no light at the end of the tunnel. To be sure, none of these moments of failure is comparable to the depth of the cosmic shut-down of that crucifixion Friday (see Matt 27:51–54; Luke 23:44–45), but we do imagine by analogue. The work of faith is the embrace of that zero hour.

Wilder has chosen the rich and suggestive verb, "*breed.*" He does not say "make" or produce," or "evoke." "Breed" suggests something organic to the zero hour that is itself generative of the possible we have taken to be impossible. The Bible does not use the verb "breed," but in Numbers 11:12, Moses suggests that YHWH has "conceived" Israel; see Isaiah 49:15 as well. Thus, the notion of "breed" is not far from the way in which the Bible speaks of the emergence of the inexplicably new. For the male party in the birth process the verb is "beget," and for the female we get "birth." In the pairing of "beget" and "birth" we get something like "breed," a hidden, inscrutable, inexplicable emergence of new life that is impelled we know not how. The Bible is perforce reticent about the process, but clearly understands that hidden emergence of new life is within the governance of God's holiness. It is for that reason that Isaiah can have God voiced in the specificity of the quotidian process of birthing:

> For a long time I have held my peace,
> I have kept still and restrained myself;
> now I will cry out like a woman in labor,
> I will gasp and pant. (Isa 42:14)

85

The Bible does not and cannot explain the breeding process, but marvels at it:

> By faith he received power of procreation, even though he was too old—and Sarah herself was barren—because he considered him faithful who had promised. Therefore, from one person, and him as good as dead, descendants were born, as many as the stars of heaven and as the innumerable grains of sand by the seashore. (Heb 11:11–12)

The capacity of God to deliver newness is given more grand doxological articulation by Paul: ". . . who gives life to the dead and calls into existence the things that do not exist" (Rom 4:17).

The capacity for newness from the zero hour is peculiarly in the gift of God.

What emerges in this hidden process, according to Wilder, is *new algebra*. The newness does not accommodate any of our old calculations or our usual explanations. What we get is a new world of reality that does not answer to our old certitudes. In the zero hour what is "bred" is a wonder that defies our old controls. The over-used word for such a wonder is miracle." That word works, however, only when we refuse the notion that it is a "violation of the natural order." No, "miracle" is a disclosure of the holiness of God, an event, says Martin Buber, that is laden with "abiding astonishment."

So consider Wilder's formulation:

- *Zero hour*: a moment without possibility;

- *Breed*: a hidden process of newness laden with holiness;

- *New algebra*: a way of configuring reality beyond all of our old certitudes.

I could think of three instances in scripture when the new algebra arrives as a surprise. (You may think of others).

In the book of Judges, Israel reaches a very low point of helplessness before the incursive power of the Midianites who violently seize their life resources. This is indeed a zero hour for ancient Israel:

> They would encamp against them and destroy the pro-
> duce of the land, as far as the neighborhood of Gaza,
> and leave no sustenance in Israel, and no sheep or ox
> or donkey. For they and their livestock would come up,
> and they would even bring their tents, as thick as locusts;
> neither they nor their camels could be counted; so they
> wasted the land as they came in. Thus Israel was greatly
> impoverished because of Midian. (Judg 6:4–6)

After some extended negotiation, Gideon is dispatched by YHWH to rescue Israel from the Midianite threat:

> Then the LORD turned to him and said, "Go in this might
> of yours and deliver Israel from the hand of Midian; I
> hereby commission you." (v. 14)

Gideon can do the numbers quite well. He knows that Israel is outnumbered and outmanned for any challenge to the Midianites:

> But sir, how can I deliver Israel? My clan is the weakest in
> Manasseh, and I am the least in my family. (v. 16)

But after he is given assurance of YHWH's backing, he issues a general order of mobilization to all the tribes. The call to recruit was effective, in all; 32,000 men. Gideon adheres to Colin Powell's doctrine of "massive force." The number could be overwhelming for the coming confrontation. There is, however, a catch:

> Then the LORD said to Gideon: The troops with you are
> too many for me to give the Midianites into their hand.
> Israel will only take the credit away from me, saying, "My
> own hand has delivered me." (7:2)

Such huge numbers would remove any hint of vulnerability and detract credit from YHWH who has pledged to save Israel. Consequently, Gideon, in response to YHWH's insistence, pares down his number of troops. He sent away the fearful:

> Thus Gideon sifted them out; twenty-two thousand re-
> turned, and ten thousand remained. (v. 3)

He is very good at numbers! That, however, does not yet satisfy YHWH:

> The troops are still too many. (7: 4)

Gideon is acting by the old calculus. But this zero hour with the Midianites evokes from YHWH a new algebra that Gideon must finally embrace. By the use of the wisdom of guerilla war the number of troops is cut to three hundred. That new algebra in which Gideon is instructed turns out well in the end with only three hundred warriors:

> They seized the waters as far as Bethbarah, and also the Jordan. They captured the two captains of Midian, Oreb and Zeeb; they killed Oreb at the rock of Oreb, and Zeeb they killed at the wine press of Zeeb, they pursued the Midianites. They brought the heads of Oreb and Zeeb to Gideon beyond the Jordan. (7:24–25)

No one could have foreseen the outcome of the zero hour; the new algebra has prevailed!

An even more spectacular case of the new algebra is narrated in 2 Kings 6:8–23. In this zero hour for Samaria, the threat of Aram (Syria) is acute. The king of Syria regards Elisha as an intelligence "leaker" and so surrounds his home with his threatening troops. As Elisha's attendant is alert to the danger of this threat, he cries out in fear, "Alas, master, what shall we do?" v. 16). The guy can count: Two of us, a host of them! Elisha, however, is a master of the new algebra: "Do not be afraid, for there are more with us than there are with them" (v. 16). His servant is quite bewildered because he lives by the old math. He knows that "two" is a very small number. He wonders about "more with us." How could that be? But then the servant has his eyes wondrously opened to what could be seen only when YHWH gives vision. He was able to "do the numbers" in a fresh, very different way:

> So the LORD opened the eyes of the servant, and he saw: the mountain was full of horses and chariots of fire all around Elisha. (2 Kgs 6:17)

The hidden resources of God were decisive in moving Israel beyond the zero hour of threat to a new algebra. That new algebra, for Elisha, ended in a "great feast" that for an instant turned an enemy into a neighbor (v. 24).

Among the most spectacular instances of the new algebra on the horizon of Christians is the twice reiterated narrative of food. The zero hour was that a great crowd was in the wilderness that was "like sheep without a shepherd" (Mark 6:34), "without anything to eat" (8:1). The "breeding" of the new algebra, for Jesus, was that he was "moved with compassion" (6:34; 8:2). That is, his innards were in turmoil with the urgent need he saw. In response to that desperate need, he took from the crowd five loaves and two fish" (6:38), "some bread" and "a few small fish" (8:5–7). He performed his dominical act in four steps:

> He took,
> > he blessed,
> > > he broke,
> > > > he gave.

The outcome of that "breeding" moment was variously twelve baskets of surplus bread for the twelve tribes of Israel (6:43) or seven loaves of bread for the stereotypical "seven nations" (8:8), that is, in both case, ample for all! The disciples had of course not understood: "How can one feed these people with bread here in the desert?" (8:4). How could such a small amount of food feed so many? What they then glimpsed, well beyond their expectation or explanation, was the new algebra of abundance. And when the church reperforms that "breeding moment" of his four transformative verbs, we are led to the new algebra. Every time we remember and participate, moreover, we are recruited into the new algebra that supersedes and defies the old math of parsimony.

And now, we are heirs of Gideon, Elisha, and Jesus—always again learning the new algebra while we remain stuck in the old math. The old math is informed by fear, scarcity, greed, and hostility. The old rule is a practice of "doing the numbers" according to shortage and surplus, predation and vulnerability. We have had, twice, glimpses of the new algebra in ample bread, and every once in a while we observe its transformative practice among us.

Just now, surely, in the midst of the virus we are at a defining zero hour in our society and in the world. That zero hour evokes fear, anger, and even hoarding. In that moment of fear, anger, and hoarding, however, when we have eyes to see, we see the new algebra working the numbers in fresh ways. In the new algebra, the silenced and the invisible among us count. In the new algebra, there is no parsimony in the face of deep bodily need. Through the new algebra we may notice the emergence of new neighborly policies that treat others like neighbors. The old rule continues to have a deep grasp on our imagination. As a result, we are fearful that someone somewhere will get something for nothing. In the old math, we regard "mine" as "mine," not ever to be shared. In the old math, we protect privilege and advantage. But the new breeding goes on in spite of us! And then, from time to time, we are amazed as was Gideon, as was the servant of Elisha, as were the disciples and the crowds around Jesus. Amos Wilder would have us do the numbers. But the numbers, in the new algebra:

- let 300 with Gideon prevail against a large military host;
- let Elisha and his servant, these two, host a transformative feast;
- let the 5000 and the 4000 feast on five loaves and a few small fish.

Those numbers get our attention and cause us to marvel: 300, two, and five loaves with two fish that eventuate in victory, feast, and surplus bread! The numbers evoke in us wonder. It is a wonder that the holy generosity of God is not contained in our conventional arithmetic. It is, moreover, a wonder when we are so inured in the old math and yet are invited beyond our calculations.

Jesus conducts a review session with his disciples so that they can engage the new algebra:

> When I broke the five loaves for the five thousand, how many baskets full of broken pieces did you collect?" They

said to him, "Twelve." And the seven for the four thousand, how many baskets full of broken pieces did you collect?" And they said to him, "Seven." Then he said to them, "Do you not understand?" (Mark 6:52)

I suspect that if Amos Wilder had narrated this exchange he would have had Jesus ask, "Do you not yet understand about the new algebra?"

Prerequisite of great faith.
The power of love & prayer

13

Turn, Change, Remember

THE NARRATIVE OF THE "golden calf" stands as a paradigmatic tale of Israel's skewed covenant with YHWH. Excluding the Priestly instruction of Exodus 25–31, this story in Exodus 32 follows *immediately* after the covenant-making in Exodus 24. There is not even the space of a breath between *covenant-making* and *covenant-breaking!*

The breaking of the covenant in this story is because Israel yearns for and must have an immediately available God. Israel cannot tolerate the holiness of YHWH that marks God with freedom—the freedom to be absent, remote, or inaccessible. (N.B. Our all-too-ready eagerness to assure believers among us that God is *ever present* and *on call* is sobered by this narrative!). Because the holy God of Sinai is not immediately available the God-maker, Aaron must get to work. Aaron is a priestly theological type, so he knows what to do. He knows how to "make" and "make available" a God who is able and willing to respond to Israel's religious hunger. This narrative is about God-making that responds to the yearning of religious neediness.

All you need to make in order to make a god is a measure of the substance that is most valuable in the community, in this case *gold*. Along with gold all you need is a *mold* that can shape the gold. The mold readily available to Aaron is a calf, well, better a "bull." The "calf" is symbol and embodiment of virility and fertility, the strength, power, and capacity to generate new life! All you need to make a god is a little gold, a pattern of vitality and fertility that bespeaks self-sufficiency, and some *imagination* to see how a precious commodity can be made (formed) into a compelling, reassuring, ever present, ever available god. This compelling, reassuring, ever present, ever available god is such a welcome alternative to the demanding, uncompromising, sometimes absent holy God of Sinai. Thus *gold* imagined into a *bull* is so attractive because it is divinized version of our own best, most powerful self in our generative capacity to make, order, govern, and control life on our own terms. It is not for nothing that the image a gold-bull is the defining icon of Wall Street, the great venue of self-sufficient wealth, power, and control. Wall Street is the lens of wealth and power that controls the economy, that has for a long time mobilized cheap labor (through bondaging debt), and by market expansion and by deployment of troops has reached the extremes of the earth for ever greater wealth. This passion for god-making is reiterated by our ready commoditization of the world, our reduction of all of life to a tradable commodity that issues in control.

The reiteration of the narrative in the Psalm declares:

> They exchanged the glory of God
>> for the image of an ox that eats grass.
> They forget God their Savior,
>> who had done great things in Egypt. (Ps 106:20–21)

The calf/bull has become an "ox." But that is all the same when it comes to "breeding" self-sufficiency. Israel (Aaron) traded God's majestic glory for a mere creature that could be tamed and worked, a calf! Such a "trade" is only possible because of their wholesale forgetting. The Israelites forgot their narrative of emancipation. They could no longer remember their cruel slavery from which they had been rescued. They forgot because they had become safe and secure from all alarms. What we know is that *affluence* begets *amnesia:*

> When your herds and flocks have multiplied, and your
> silver and gold is multiplied, and all that you have is mul-
> tiplied . . . Do not say to yourself, "My power and the
> might of my own hand have gotten me this wealth. But
> remember the LORD your God, for it is he who gives you
> power to get wealth. (Deut 8:13–18)

In a circumstance of security and property, it is easy and convenient to scuttle old memories of bondage, impotence, and despair
and the inexplicable gift of emancipation. In amnesia one can then
exult in self-sufficiency, incapable of remembering being vulnerable and having been given of new life. Thus the "forgetting" of
Israel is not mere absent-mindedness. It is a willful act to expel
memories that define our lives as other than as autonomous and
self-made.

But, of course, such willful amnesia will not work. It will
not work because self-sufficiency is unsustainable. In the most
elemental ways we do not initiate our lives; we are on the receiving
end of good gifts. For good reason, Paul can ask:

> What do you have that you did not receive as a gift? And
> if you received it, why do you boast as if it were not a gift?
> (1 Cor 4:7)

It is all gift! It is all the gift of God. It all properly evokes gratitude that is expressed as neighborly generosity. When gifts are
transposed into achievements, accomplishments, and possessions,
however, gratitude evaporates, generosity vanishes, and neighbors
become invisible.

It will not work! It did not take long for the holy God to notice the willful illusionary defiance of Israel via Aaron. Even from
a distance the holy God can spot such perversity. It is a perversity
that must have seemed to Aaron only a new celebrative religiosity.
But God's ways are not Aaron's ways! God will have none of it. Karl
Barth puts it succinctly:

> Such was the breach of the covenant in Ex 2—man as
> the *creator Dei*, self-controlling and self-sufficient and

self-defying man, the man of sin in this first form of pride.[1]

One can concluded that the "new normal" authorized by the golden bull of affluent successful self-sufficiency is the order of the day among us. After all, US exceptionalism serves such a claim. White supremacy makes the same claim. An even more generic sense of entitlement reaches out to both conservatives and liberals. Such prideful self-regard has no room for the holy God who refuses our self-congratulatory mood. So how might God's holiness undo such self-congratulatory life? Well, by rendering our self-sufficiency as penultimate and inadequate. Right now we are living with the failure of our most secure institutions as we watch the undoing of our taken-for-granted world. No one (certainly not this one!) would ever say that the virus is divine judgment. But then, the undoing of a world of recalcitrance is not likely to be direct or intrusive. The undoing is more likely to appear in an invisible but real pressure on our ordinary living. The outcome is our humbling that is not overcome by loud protest, phony piety, or illusionary posturing. We have a time in which to be a humble, receptive people if we have courage enough to notice.

But this tale of sad humbling at the hand of the holy God has a swerve to it. The same Moses who is privy to God's anger toward perverse Israel is the Moses who now speaks up to counter God's self-satisfied intention to punish. As a result this is not simply a story of *sin and judgment*, though it is that. After the straight-forward simplicity of sin and judgment, the narrative is made more complex and more interesting by the response of Moses as a third party to the drama. Moses interrupts what scholars call the "lawsuit" of *indictment and sentence*. Moses dares to question the appropriateness and wisdom God's anger. This daring interruption by Moses is so deeply Jewish! It would not happen among conventional Christians, because conventional Christians are excessively pious and deferential. But Moses is resolutely Jewish in this moment of covenantal engagement. He knows that he can (and must!)

1. Barth, *Church Dogmatics* IV/1, 432.

address God and call God to account. He puts two questions to God:

> Why be angry with this people that you have made and saved?
> Why give ammunition to the Egyptians?

Bad idea to get angry with your own people whom you love! *Bad idea* to provide the Egyptians with evidence of failure toward your own historical project! The two questions of Moses remain unanswered as though YHWH needs time to ponder. Without waiting, Moses promptly issues three imperatives to God. Yes, imperatives!

> *Turn* . . . from your anger;
> *Change* . . . your mind;
> *Remember* . . . the book of Genesis.

What a demand Moses makes to YHWH: *Turn, change, remember!* The exchange ends laconically without inflection:

> And the LORD changed his mind about the disaster that
> he planned to bring on his people. (Exod 32:14)

Evidently YHWH takes the imperatives and the questions of Moses seriously. Moses prevailed! God is talked out of God's immense anger!

I conclude that the accent of our interpretation is not on either *the sin of Aaron* or on *the anger of God*. What matters are the courage of Moses and the readiness of Moses to call God to account, to summon God back the matrix of promise. The psalm says, "Moses stood in the breach." I am not sure I want to draw any practical learning from this account. If I did, however, it would be to insist that Moses (and his ilk after Moses) is not identified with the transgression of Aaron. We know better than that. Moses did not participate in the folly of Aaron. But we know as well that Moses is not identified with the holy wrath of YHWH. Moses himself displays no anger at the action of Aaron. Moses, rather, has a distinct and different role to play in this crisis of pride and humbling. The ilk of Moses after him is to play a distinctive role in the drama of pride and humbling. We, after Moses, may do so with intense intercessions that summon God to God's best most faithful self as did Moses. Beyond that, the work in the drama is to mediate life *beyond pride* (that has failed) and *beyond humbling* (that has been for the most part withheld. This move "beyond" is a bet on the future, a conviction that God and God's people are meant to have together a better practice in a better circumstance.

Thus by the end of chapter 32 Moses bids God for forgiveness (v. 32). Our society is in great need of forgiveness that it cannot manufacture for itself, forgiveness for a brutal history, for its brazen racism, for its uncaring autonomy, for its assumption of elected privilege, and for its illusionary sufficiency. Of course! After that, however, at the end of the narrative God moves on:

> But now go, lead the people to the place about which I have spoken to you; see, my angel shall go in front of you. (v. 34)

The promise of God to Israel persists.

The mandate is to move to a new and better place. The work of Moses, in light of this sad exchange, is to lead God's people to "the land of promise." The people dancing around the golden bull would have thought they had already arrived at the land promise (see v. 8). It is always so with those who have "arrived" or think they have arrived. But not so! Thus affluent self-sufficiency, safe and secure from all alarms, is not the land of promise. The land of promise is the place where the commandments of God are readily and gladly embraced, where God is loved above all else, where neighbors are loved like ourselves. That new land of wellbeing requires *new imagination*. It requires *new attitudes*. It requires *new policies*. It requires *new practices*. This is all the work of this third party who exercises courageous agency in the breach. In chapter 34 the covenant is remade. It can be remade by God's initiative because:

> The LORD is merciful and gracious,
>   slow to anger and abounding in steadfast love.
> He will not always accuse,

> nor will he keep his anger forever.
> He does not deal with us according to our sins,
> nor repay us according to our iniquities.
> (Ps 103:8–10; see Exod 34:6)

This remaking of the covenant is the work of Moses. It is his hard work to negotiate, to coax both parties back to the covenant, to coax God back to generosity and to coax Israel back to responsibility. That is the good work of Moses. It is work that is not yet finished among us, work that is an urgent vocation.

14

Food Secure!

I am "food secure"! I eat out frequently in the lovely venues in my town, Red Ginger, Poppycock, Harrington's by the Bay, or West End Tavern. I would not have known to use that phrase for myself except that I hear much talk in our town of disproportionate wealth about the "food insecure." Indeed my own church daily feeds a meal to over a hundred "food insecure" "neighbors," some of whom are homeless, though not all. It is such an odd juxtaposition in our town between the "food insecure" and those of us who are luxuriously "food secure" without even noticing that we are, or reflecting on it. Indeed, it is "normal" in our time to take our food security for granted while we only occasionally (if at all!) notice the "food insecure" who enjoy all the benefits of poor housing and low wages.

This juxtaposition of the "food secure" and the "food insecure" is not new. It is the story of organized humanity. James C. Scott has traced from the beginning of political economy the way in which the powerful were able to organize a monopoly of "grain" and so could administer food resources according to the whims and interests of the powerful.[1] This capacity to administer grain

1. Scott, *Against the Grain*.

supplies is of course evident in the Bible in the "storehouse cities" of Pharaoh (Exod 1:11; see Gen 47:13–19), and then the "storehouse cities" of King Solomon (1 Kgs 9:19; 2 Chr 8:4–6). In ancient Israel the economy was organized according to *subsistence* for the agricultural peasants and *luxury* for the urban elites who managed the state economy for the sake of their surplus.[2]

We get glimpses of the luxury of the "food secure" in Israel. King Solomon presided over an extravagant meat-eating household:

> Solomon's provision for one day was thirty cors of choice flour, and sixty cors of meal, ten fat oxen, and twenty pasture-fed cattle, one hundred sheep, besides deer, gazelles, roebucks, and fatted fowl. (1 Kgs 4:22–23)

Imagine the royal apparatus that made such extravagance possible! And imagine how much grain was required to produce all that meat! Later on Amos could castigate those "at ease in Zion" and those "feel secure" [sic!] in Mt. Samaria (Amos 6:1). Zion (Jerusalem) and Samaria were the two capitol cities, the citadels of money and power where the controlling vehicles of the state resided:

> Alas for those who lie on beds of ivory,
>   and lounge on their couches,
> and eat lambs from the flock,
>   and calves from the stall. (Amos 6:4)

Their meat supply is limitless. The deep affront of the "food secure" is this:

> They are not grieved over the ruin of Joseph. (v. 6)

They did not notice! They did not see that the common life of the community was a "ruin" because of disastrous food policy and practice. They were so sated that their diet had numbed them to social reality. Thus Solomon (in the tenth century BCE) and Amos (in the eighth century BCE) sketch out the "food secure."

Sandwiched between them Elisha (in the ninth century BCE) performs a very different food narrative! In 2 Kings 4:42–44 we

2. On this, see Boer, *The Sacred Economy of Ancient Israel.*

are offered a glimpse into this remarkable capacity on behalf of the "food insecure." He took modest measures of grain and barley; he fed a hundred hungry people and had some left over. The narrative is terse. No explanation is offered, only an affirmation that Elisha, outside the royal protocols of scarcity, has food-generating capacity.

In the midst of a severe food shortage, Elisha performs a very different strategy (2 Kgs 6:24—7:20). It is important to note that a "famine" does not mean there is no food. Rather it means that scarce food makes the price of food very expensive, beyond the reach of the disadvantage. This we are told:

> A donkey's head was sold for eighty shekels of silver, and one-fourth of a kab of dove's dung for five shekels of silver. (6:25)

It is no wonder that the left behind must scramble for food, in this case two women who are desperately hungry. In the face of such an emergency, Elisha is unflinching in his anticipation:

> Tomorrow about this time a measure of choice meal shall be sold for a shekel, and two measures of barley for a shekel, at the gate of Samaria. (7:1)

The royal captain, inured to scarcity for the masses, resists such an anticipation of food at cheap prices (7:2). But Elisha is uncompromising in his assurance. The narrative tells of the recovery of food from the enemy (Syrian) military camp as the enemy had fled in a panic. Discovery of this unexpected food supply is regarded by the lepers (those excluded from the resources of the royal regime) as good news (gospel news!) (7:9). In the end, the prophet is vindicated in his expectation of ample cheap food. It was remembered that he had promised:

> Two measures of barley shall be sold for a shekel, and a measure of choice meal for a shekel, about this time tomorrow in the gate of Samaria. (7:18)

The royal captain is excluded from the new food supply, because he is committed to a scarcity model in the service of the governing regime. He is trampled by the food-hungry peasants (7:20)! Now the "people" and the two women can eat, not at all dependent on the royal regime with its protocols of scarcity. Elisha has effected a game-changer!

In a third narrative of Elisha we are told of the durable hostility between Israel and Syria (2 Kgs 6:8–23). The prophet prevents the desire of the Israelite king to kill the enemy. Instead of such a vengeful killing he issues a very different imperative:

> Set food and water before them so that they may eat and drink; and let them go to their master. (v. 22)

We are told that the cycle of violent brutality was broken by this surprising offer of food:

> He sent them on their way, and they went to their master.
> And the Arameans no longer came raiding into the land
> of Israel. (v. 23)

This generous unmerited offer of food to an enemy broke the cycle of fear and hostility. The prophet understood that food is a vehicle for reconciliation. Against the war-mongering of the royal apparatus, Elisha is a peace-maker and his mode is food!

In all of these narratives Elisha is presented as "a man of food." In 4:42–44 he feeds a hungry throng. In 6:24—7:20 he feeds the people and dispatches a resistant captain of the king. In 6:22–23 he breaks the cycle of violence by food. All of these acts depend upon an alternative management of food. All of these acts take place in defiance of the royal regime that had settled for scarcity. The narrative does not explain; it only witnesses to the odd way in which food can outflank the royal regime that in its scarcity could do nothing about food. Indeed the king was willing to settle for "food insecurity" for his people. These narratives serve to make Elisha the heir of the manna story of Exodus 16. In that narrative Israel could remember there was ample bread. Beyond the supply of Pharaoh and his predatory policies, food is given! Loaves abound! And now Elisha, in the face of the scarcity regime, performs abundance!

Food Secure!

When we fast forward we can see that Jesus reiterates the wonders of abundance wrought by Elisha. He also encountered a hungry crowd in the wilderness (Mark 6:30–44). He had compassion on them. The Greek term for "compassion" indicates a troubled stirring of Jesus' innards. His body was vexed when he saw their desperate hunger. Like Elisha before him, Jesus took a little and performed maximum food for 5000 men. The process of performing such abundance consisted in his four great verbs:

He took the loaves and fish;
He blessed them;
He broke them;
He gave them.

By "taking" and "giving" Jesus subjects these bits of food to his lordly will for abundance. Like Elisha Jesus lives and works outside the protocols of scarcity that regularly gives some surplus and leaves others bereft. Amid his abundance, all ate; all were filled. The abundance was so great that there was left over from his lordly act twelve baskets of bread, enough for all the tribes of Israel.

After the Syrophoenician woman had reprimanded him for his limited horizon and his provincialism (Mark 7:24–30), Jesus reperformed his abundance (Mark 8:1–10). Again he meets a hungry crowd. Again he is stirred to compassion. Again he does his four transformative verbs, only this time "he blessed" has become "he gave thanks" (*eucharistesas*). Again the crowd, this time four thousand people, ate and were filled. This time there were seven baskets of bread as surplus, enough for the conventional roster of "seven nations;" It would have pleased the Syrophoenician women that this time in the wake of her reprimand, the surplus of abundance as designed for the nations! This is indeed Bread for the World!

In these acts Jesus, like Elisha, changed the world. The "food insecure" were treated with dignity and provided enough they were able, for now, to be "food secure." The work of abundance is to move the neighbors who are food insecure into the circle of those who are food secure. These acts of abundance do not make everyone equal. But they do open the prospect for the abundant life.

The work of abundance continues in the world. It turns out, moreover, that virus time has become a time for abundance that underwrites new food security along with other forms of security as well. It is amazing that in this time many people have willingly stepped outside protocols of scarcity that have seemed so sacrosanct, and have signed on for the generosity that is transformative.

I cite only one remarkable case of such abundance. Camden, New Jersey, which has a past marked by great social conflict, has now witnessed an extraordinary act of abundance. Instead of the police being, as in the past, adversaries of protesters, the police this time responded differently and stood with the protesters. Most remarkably the report of the protest and police encounter ends this way:

> At the conclusion of Saturday's demonstration, police held what they call a pop-up barbecue for residents, including hot dogs, hamburgers, and a Mister Softee ice cream truck. Officers are doing more barbecues on Sunday. (June 1, 2020 in *New York Times*)

Police Chief Joe Wysocki commented:

> There's no alternative. We can't impose our will on a community. It's the community and police together, and that's what we're doing in Camden.

The action of the police strikes one as closely parallel to the action of Elisha toward the Syrian enemy. The offer of food turns enemies into potential neighbors.

The call of Jesus' new governance is to step outside the protocols of scarcity, and to refuse to be defined by them. It turns out that "scarcity" is not a given in the world. It is, rather, a construct proposed by those who do not want to share, who would rather have the "food insecure" as enemies rather than neighbors. Being "food secure" could of course be an outcome of wealth and success. Or it could be an action of neighborliness wherein all eat and all are filled. Ours is a time when we are witnessing the possibility that the protocols of scarcity had declared to be impossible. Every time the church performs its wonder of bread and wine and gives thanks (Eucharist!), it affirms its confidence in the abundance of God that subverts our assumed scarcity.

15

For Terry

Upon the death of Terry Fretheim Old Testament study has lost a great force, for Terry was a powerful, influential shaper of our discipline. For a generation, since the publication of his groundbreaking book, *The Suffering of God* (1984),[1] he has led the way in our work. In his death theological education has lost a great teacher, for Terry had a way of engaging students without imposing conclusions on them. And the church has lost a great pastor, for Terry's pastoral sensibility was always apparent to those around him.

Beyond all of that, I have lost a great friend. Terry was my longest-running conversation partner in Old Testament study. He and I, both rooted in the best traditions of German pietism, were twinned together in much of our work. Early on in the commentary series, Interpretation, Terry wrote *Exodus* and I wrote *Genesis*. Later on in *The New Interpreter's Bible* we reversed the work; he wrote *Genesis* and I wrote *Exodus*. Over time, enough difference between us emerged to evoke an ongoing conversation about the ways in which the Old Testament bears witness to the action of God in the world.

1 Fretheim, *The Suffering of God*.

Through his focus on creation themes Terry drew the conclusion that God's work in the world was a part of an ongoing process; thus he was attracted to the categories of Process Theology. He judged, moreover, that in the governance of history God's action was characteristically in and through historical agents, and not directly. Thus, for example, mighty Assyria could be "the rod of my anger" (Isa 10:5), and Cyrus the Persian king could be the "messiah" (Isa 45:1).

Conversely, my attention was especially drawn to the emancipation narratives of the Old Testament that I have read through a liberation hermeneutic. Through that lens God is portrayed as being the help of the helpless when "other helpers fail and comforts flee." Consequently, as in the Exodus narrative, God is seen to act through direct agency.

Terry's judgment was that I had been excessively influenced by the "strong God" of John Calvin whom he thought had overstated the direct agency of God. Conversely, I thought Terry, in his embrace of a process hermeneutic, had given away too much of the direct agency of God as sovereign. Surely there are enough biblical texts to argue in either direction, and so our exchange was left without resolution. It is likely, moreover, that our different interpretive stances were complexly formed by our theological upbringing, by our personalities, and by our social locations.

It is likely that Terry had the better of that argument, given how it is that God is known in the world. However our shared wonderment might have been resolved, I am glad to add the following as a tribute and a salute to my dear friend. I want to consider the remarkable characterization of God in Deuteronomy 10:14–18. These verses in the mouth of Moses articulate the glorious mystery of God whom Israel knows in majesty and in mercy. At the outset of this doxology it is affirmed that all of heaven, all of earth, and all of earth's creatures belong to God (v. 14). The arresting "yet" of verse 15 reverses field and affirms God's peculiar singular commitment to Israel alone, both its ancestors and its descendants. The interface of cosmic governance in verse 14 and singular love in verse 15 marks the wonder of biblical faith. That same move from majesty to mercy is reiterated in verses 17 and 18. In verse 17, the majestic sovereignty of YHWH is affirmed in a striking doxology. But then in verse 18, the attentive reach of YHWH's rule concerns widows, orphans, and strangers for whom the necessities of life (food and clothing) are provided by YHWH. Moses readily affirms that the majestic rule of God pivots in attentive care for the forgotten and the excluded.

We—Terry and I—may ask, "How is it that God gives bread?" We know of course about the manna narrative in which God's bread simply appears for Israel in the wilderness as the dew lifts in the morning:

> When the layer of dew lifted, there on the surface of the wilderness was a fine flaky substance as fine as frost on the ground. (Exod 16:14)

When Moses is queried about the wondrous bread, he answered:

> It is the bread that the LORD has given you to eat. (v. 15; see Pss 78:20; 105:40)

The affirmation explains nothing, because God's gift of bread is beyond explanation. We know, moreover, of the doxological exuberance of Isaiah concerning the faithfulness of God:

> For as the rain and the snow come down from heaven,
>   and do not return there until they have watered the earth,
> making it bring forth and sprout,
>   giving seed to the sower and *bread to the eater* ... (Isa 55:10)

And in YHWH's commitment to Zion it is promised:

> I will abundantly bless its provisions;
>   I will *satisfy its poor with bread.* (Ps 132:15)

Israel is not reluctant in its recognition that God gives bread, just as Moses had declared.

These affirmations, however, tell us nothing about how bread from the creator God is given in the earth. In my conversations with Terry, I had been content to let those claims of bread from God stand as they are, without further explanation. Terry, however, would readily press the point to ask, how that bread is to be delivered. He would likely call attention to the next verse in Deuteronomy 10:19. After Moses makes his sweeping claim for God, the next verse moves, as covenantal faith always does, to an imperative:

> You (plural) shall also love the stranger. (v. 19)

Israel had been a stranger (immigrant) in Egypt; and should therefore be attentive to the needs of other strangers (immigrants). And from that single mandate, we can freely extrapolate other mandates I take to be tacit in the utterance of Moses:

> You shall also love the widow;
>> You shall also love the orphan;
>>> You shall be sure to execute justice;
>>> You shall provide clothing;
>>> You shall provide bread.

Terry would surely conclude that God's gift of bread is given through human agency.

So how is God's bread given in the world?

- Bread is given through *governmental policy*. In the ancient world the king had an obligation to provide food for the hungry (see 2 Kgs 6:16). In current US policy, food is provided through the food stamp program of the Department of Agriculture. Many persons rely on that provision, even if Secretary of Agriculture, Sonny Purdue, is parsimonious in his fear that someone will "become dependent" on such food. Imagine becoming dependent on a reliable food supply! Perdue's gut fear no doubt is that someone will get something for free, alas!

- Bread is given through *a host of NGOs*. We may be grateful for the lobbying efforts of such agencies as Bread for the World that relentlessly pursues good food policy in its address to widespread hunger, on which see *Hunger: the Oldest Problem* by Martin Caparrós.

- Bread is given through the efforts of *a myriad of volunteers,* often organized through the church, to provide food for the food deprived. In my community an organization of volunteers provides a daily truck circuit to pick up large amounts of surplus food for distribution in a variety of local venues. Among the many diligent, committed, hard-working volunteers in such enterprises is the indefatigable Mary Brown, who presides over a creative blog platform.

On all these counts—*government policy, action organizations,* and *local volunteers*—the bread given by God is made available through human agency. Terry would have no doubt that it is God who gives bread. But Terry would also insist that bread from God is not magical or supernatural. It is rather the faithful, proper functioning of the human community that makes bread available; it is a human performance of mercy, compassion, and generosity that constitute the delivery system for God's good bread. Thus as we pray for "daily bread," we may also be grateful for the actions of human governments, human organizations, and human volunteers who function to deliver that daily bread, most especially among those who possess no bread supply of their own.

For good reason I am glad to recognize that Terry, in his honed theological sensibility, is surely right about God's gift via human agency. Such a recognition on my part simply adds to the awareness that we all have that Terry has been among us a shrewd and discerning interpreter. He understood that bread is an important indispensable part of the ongoing process whereby creation is sustained and fed. Terry for good reason made a great deal out of the creation hymn of Psalm 104 that sings out:

> You cause the grass to grow for the cattle,
>   and plants for people to use,
> to bring forth food from the earth,
>   and wine to gladden the heart,
> oil to make the face shine,
>   and *bread to strengthen the human heart.*
>   (vv. 14–15)

For Terry

Terry was endlessly my teacher who would not let me get by with anything, and certainly not with careless thinking about texts I had overlooked. His great legacy will continue to teach us for many years. And we, in his wake, will be alert to the processive power and beauty of creation. He has vigorously reminded us of our vocation in creation that has been entrusted to us:

> God's way into the future with this creation is dependent at least in part on what human beings do and say. This state of affairs brings human responsibility to the forefront of the conversation. Many of us would just as soon leave everything up to God, and God can then be blamed when things go wrong, tragically or otherwise. A way between pessimism in the face of the difficulties on the one hand and a Messiah complex on the other will not always be easy to locate. But God calls human beings to take up these God-given tasks with insight and energy—for the sake of God's world and all its creatures, indeed for God's sake.[2]

Of course, I do not know what Terry's vocation is to be in "the age to come." But I do know that he will perform faithfully, through his assignment, the rule of the God of justice whom he knew to be the God of mercy.

[handwritten note]

---

2. Fretheim, *God and World in the Old Testament*, 277–78.

16

Possibility and Reality

THE "THREE/ONE" VISITOR DECLARED to Sarah and Abraham that they would have a son and heir in their old age. Having a son was for them in their old age an impossibility. Sarah giggled at the impossibility. Before they departed the "three/one" visitor posed a question to the aged couple: "*Is anything impossible for God?*" The question is left unanswered in the narrative. It is, moreover, left unanswered so that people of faith should be durably haunted by the question. It is still for us a haunting question: "Is anything impossible for God?"

Early on in his great *Church Dogmatics* I/2, Karl Barth pauses over the tricky relationship between *possibility* and *reality*.[1] He observes that when we begin with the "possible," we reduce "reality" to that which fits our idea of the "possible." And when we define the "possible" according to the requirements of modern reason we end up with a very truncated notion of "reality," including the "reality" of God. Thus if we conform to modern Enlightenment rationality, the "possible" will seem to us only what is that modern logic can allow. If, however, we begin with the "reality" of our faith and our confession of the freedom of God, our embrace of

1. Barth, *Church Dogmatics* I/2, 1–10.

the "possible" is opened up well beyond modern logic. Thus at the outset Barth sees that we must resist beginning with our notions of the "possible" and begin with the gospel reality of creation and Easter that permit and require a very different shaping and imagining of the "possible." Thus in the Genesis 18 narrative Sarah and Abraham have decided that an old couple cannot have a child: it is not possible! But the question of the visitor intends to challenge that assumption and at least leave open the chance that what the old couple took to be impossible is, by the faithfulness of God, fully possible. The visitors do not press the point and do not foreclose the question. They do, however, leave it open for Sarah and Abraham, and for us.

We might begin our reflection on this text with the recognition that the notion of the "possible" among us is defined by our best scientific learning, by our most trusted experience, by our best logic, by our most advanced technological capacity, and above all by our reckoning through the capitalist economy. We can recognize, then, that the "possible" has clearly defined limitations. So let us imagine that people (including the preacher) come to worship with a tacit awareness of all of these limits. And then in the context of Christian liturgy, these other affirmations are mouthed: "The Lord is risen." "You are forgiven." "He's got the whole world in his hands." According to the logic with which many of us come to church, all of this is "impossible." But in church we appeal to "reality" that lies beyond the limits of our "possible. Thus the Christian liturgy (and all parts of the life of the church) constitute a practice wherein the "possible" is recharacterized by appeal to "reality" that will not be contained in that "possible" with which we arrived. It is no wonder that Christian practice puts us in crisis about the assumed "possible" with which we arrived. It was just so for Sarah and Abraham. Their "possible" was shaken by the question. The Bible is the story of the way in which that haunting question continues to jar our best assurances about the possible in a world that is limited by our experience, logic, learning, economics, and ideology.

Because the conviction of gospel "reality" that places in jeopardy all of our notions of what is possible has been peculiarly entrusted to the church, the church is a venue for attesting the new possibility that the world judges to be impossible. Because of the task of bearing witness to the "impossible become possible," the church is inherently subversive, surprising, and transformative. When the church is contained in conventional notions of the possible, every part of its life becomes anemic:

- *The prayers of the church become anemic.* They are deferential and cautious about daring to ask for much and reluctant to tell the truth before God and to God.

- *The preaching of the church becomes anemic* and contained in what conventional society will accept, variously moralistic, sentimental, or just clever and entertaining.

- And when the prayers and preaching of the church are anemic, it is predictable that *the mission of the church will likewise become anemic*, remaining in the safe boundaries of social convention, but without transformative energy and without courage for any new question concerning justice and mercy.

The anemic practice of the church becomes a close parallel to the anemic expectation of Sarah and Abraham who are ready to live within the bounds of settled society.

The question left open by the visitor for Sarah and Abraham lingers in the Jesus story as well. Jesus becomes so dangerous to settled society because he refused conventional characterizations of what is possible. When he summarizes his work for John, moreover, he offers an inventory of transformative actions that lie outside conventional possibility:

> The blind receive their sight, the lame walk, the lepers are cleansed, the deaf hear, the dead are raised, the poor have good news brought to them. (Luke 7:22)

Nobody thought it was possible that the blind could see or that the lame could walk, or that the deaf could hear, or that the dead could be raised, or that the poor would have good news. Nobody thought any of that possible, until made possible by the performance of the new future of God in the person and presence of Jesus.

Twice in the Jesus story the question of the impossible is posed. At the outset the angel Gabriel declares to Mary the coming birth of John to Mary's kinswoman, Elizabeth:

> And now your relative Elizabeth in her old age has also conceived a son; and this is the sixth month for her who was said to be barren; for *nothing will be impossible with God*. (Luke 1:36–37)

The narrative clearly alludes to the Genesis 18 narrative. And second, after Jesus summons the man with many possessions to radical obedience, the disciples can recognize how demanding is God's new future. They despair of anyone being able to meet the requirement of the new governance. But Jesus reassures them:

> For mortals it is impossible, but not for God; *for God all things are possible*. (Mark 10:27) Wealthy enter heaven

What the world holds to be impossible is made possible by the transformative capacity of God.

There is in the Jesus narrative, however, a severe qualification is transformative capacity that I have termed a "cruciform caveat" that we cannot disregard. When Jesus prayed in the garden before he was arrested by the authorities, he prays for deliverance from his coming suffering for his obedience:

> My father, *if it is possible*, let this cup pass from me; yet not what I want but what you want. (Matt 26:39)

Even in his prayer for deliverance, however, Jesus is prepared to be fully obedient. As it turns out for Jesus, he cannot avoid his "cup of suffering" (see Mark 10:31 on the same "cup of suffering" offered to his disciples). That was not possible for him. It was an impossibility that could not be overcome. And so he suffered to death. This is the one impossibility that could not be made possible. It is not possible for Jesus (or his disciples) to live a new life in contradiction to the old world without paying a deep price. Even in its hope, the gospel is deeply honest about the matter!

We may judge that "virus time" is indeed a time for new possibilities among us:

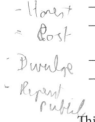

—It is time for student debt to be cancelled.
—It is time for health care to be assured to all.
—It is time for economic relief to be assigned to the unemployed.
—It is time for the waiver of insurance premiums.
—It is time to mobilize economic resources for the most needy.
—It is time to recover a passion for neighborly reality among us all.

These are all impossibilities! They are dramatic violations of the protocols of conventional capitalism. The disciples reckoned that entry through the "needle's eye" would be impossible.[2]

The question of "the possible" comes up for us acutely amid the swirl of violence amid the killing of George Floyd. We wonder whether a move beyond white racism is possible, whether the rule of justice is possible, whether a move beyond enraged violence is possible. The gospel answer to our query is possible, of course is "yes"; all things are possible. Nothing is "too hard" for the Lord of history. It is possible to move beyond white supremacy; it is possible to move beyond systemic injustice. It is possible to move beyond violence to neighborliness. *But the caveat of Gethsemane pertains!* All of this is possible, but

—not without honesty concerning our protracted history of racism;
—not without relinquishment if the privileges of whiteness so long coveted;
—not without expose of the benefits of our political, economic racism;
—not without public repentance and resolve for a new and righteous life.

This is the "impossible possibility" of the gospel for our moment to be proclaimed by the church. It is the secret route to our future, a secret laden with risk, a secret the traces the way from the Friday of violence to the Sunday of new life.

Mother Sarah and Father Abraham knew that a son for them was impossible. Such newnesses are impossibilities made possible

2. See Brown, *Through the Eye of the Needle.*

by drinking the cup of contradiction for the sake of the reality of God's coming rule among us. Such impossibilities amount to a vigorous summons to the church away from anemic prayer, anemic preaching, and anemic mission. The entire story depends upon the impossibility. It was so back in Genesis. It was so in the life of Jesus; it is so now. The future depends upon drinking "the cup" for the sake of God's coming new world among us.

17

How Long Is "a Moment"?

NOW WE DEBATE HOW long the virus will last among us. Unfortunately, that discussion has been sharply and unnecessarily politicized. On the one side, advocates for "opening up now" largely concern economic recovery and believe that the danger of the virus will be fleeting. On the other side those fearful for human safety and wellbeing imagine we are under threat for the long haul. The question of "How Long?" is an urgent one among us. The question has caused me to return to two quite peculiar verses in Isaiah in Isaiah 54:7–8 in which we have from God's own lips (via Isaiah) an acknowledgement of a season of divine abandonment. (See my comment in "Abandoned!" chap. 2 above.) Reference in the verses is to the experience of exile in which the question of "how long" was acute. The faithful wondered about the length of time in their exile as we wonder about the length of time in which we face the threat of the virus.

In this Isaiah text God provides an answer to the question. The answer is given twice:

> For a brief *moment* I abandoned you . . .
>   for a *moment* I hid my face from you. (Isa 54:7–8)

The duration of divine abandonment is "for a moment." Not long at all! The term "moment" in the text means a sudden happening, something that occurs in an instant. Thus:

> How they [the wicked] are destroyed in a *moment*,
>   swept away utterly by terrors! (Ps 73:19)

> The exulting of the wicked is short,
>   and the joy of the godless is but for a *moment*.
>   (Job 20:5)

> In a *moment* they die;
>   at midnight the people are shaken and pass away,
>   and the mighty are taken away by no human hand.
>   (Job 34:20)

> For the chastisement of my people has been greater
>   than the punishment of Sodom,
> which was overthrown in a *moment*,
>   though no hand was laid on it. (Lam 4:6)

The Hebrew term used twice in the Isaiah text (*rg'*), refers to an abrupt turn, as short as a "clap" or a "beat"; or I reckon it to be the length of time in which one can unplug an old digital clock and plug it again so quickly that it does not flash "12 12 12." In these several uses of the term, moreover, it is used for momentous negations that happen unexpectedly and inexplicably. Thus in our text, divine abandonment of Israel in exile is quite unexpected by conventional inhabitants in Jerusalem, even if the prophets had anticipated it. That divine abandonment—surely a negation—will last momentarily. Divine absence will be promptly ended, as it is assured in the second lines of verses 7 and 8. By the end of these second lines abandonment has been overcome by divine compassion. That divine abandonment will be short and will hardly appear as a blip on the screen of Israel's history or memory.

This is God's assurance to Israel in exile via Isaiah. We are offered reassuring poetic relief in the two second lines. If we reason by analogue, in our own experience, we might conclude that the durable threat of the virus will be short, over in an instant or, as our president is fond of saying, "over by the first of July." That would indeed be a divine *rg'* of the virus, a fleeting negative moment promptly overcome.

That wondrous assurance voiced by the poet offered to exiles and then belatedly to us in our crisis, moreover, is an odd match to lived reality. It is an odd match in ancient Israel because the lived reality of the exiles lasted a long time, over two generations, or reckoned properly and precisely "seventy years" (see Jer 29:10). (In fact the exile did not end abruptly at all and the homecoming from exile was a long-term transition of Jews variously coming home to Jerusalem over a long period).

I draw two conclusions. First, we know on the one hand, that the present crisis will be overcome by the good faithful power of God! The evil will end because of God. The exile will end because of God's sure compassion. The threat of the virus will end because of God's compassion. That much is sure. The God who abandons is the God who faithfully ends trouble, according to prophetic horizon. But second, the "moment" of the danger may be rendered poetically (as does Isaiah), but it must be lived bodily and historically. The exiles knew in their bodies that the deportation was not ending soon, and that they must live there in displacement a while longer (see Jer 29:4–9). In the same way, we may poetically anticipate a quick end to the threat of the virus; we know in our bodies (and in the body politic), however, that the threat of the virus is not ending soon, according to the wish-world of some; we must live prudently in the meantime for however long.

This mismatch between *poetic assurance* and *lived reality* leaves us with the question, "How long is a 'moment'?" How long is a moment in God's time? The first answer is that God's moment is not according to our clocks or our preferred schedule. That of course is how it always is with "relational time." Our time in relationships is not by the clock. Thus we may be with a loved one a long while, but because it is a treasured time it goes by much too quickly. Or we may miss a loved one, and each day of absence seems like "an eternity." Thus the "how long" of the virus, like the "how long" of the exile, can indeed be reckoned by the clock or even by the coercive requirements of the market. But it can also be calculated according to the long wait for God's compassion that sure to be granted "in a moment."

We will no doubt continue the controversy and debate amid the virus about when to "to open things up" and when "it will be safe." It is useful, in any case, to remember that we are in the time-frame of God's compassion that is secure, but not according to our eager readiness. Thus our way of reasoning in faith is congruent with the way we continue to sing, even in our readiness for a return to a more comfortable "normal":

> A thousand ages in thy sight are like an evening gone,
> short as the watch that ends the night
> before the rising sun.
> Time, like an ever rolling stream,
> bears all our years away;
> they fly forgotten, as a dream
> dies at the opening day.[1]

Time is in God's hand, all our times! For that reason we mark and measure our moments, our days, and our years very differently. The ending of the exile was in God's safe hands, and would not be terminated before God so willed it. The end of the threat of the virus is in God's safe hands, so we may continue to quarrel and debate a time line, all the while knowing that our life is from God and is back to God.

I once heard a reporter interview Willie Nelson as they walked together over Willie Nelson's golf course. The reporter, at hole #4, asked Nelson, "What is par for this hole?" Nelson answered, "Whatever I say it is." So it is in God's time: A "moment" is whatever God wills it to be. Our end of that reality over which God presides is to wait, to trust, and to obey. We do so with assurance, but with eager longing:

> For in hope we were saved. Now hope that is seen is not hope. For who hopes for what is seen? But if we hope for what we do not see, we wait for it with patience. (Rom 8:24–25)

---

1. "O God, Our Help in Ages Past," in *Glory to God*, 687.

18

God's Stunning Reversal

I NOW RETURN TO Isaiah 54:7–8 yet a third time. In "Abandoned" (chap. 2 above), I considered the fact that Israel's God-abandonment in these verses is confirmed from Gods' own lips. In "How Long Is a Moment" (chap. 17 above), I reflect on the duration of Israel's abandonment reckoned in God's own time. Now in a third reflection I consider the "resolution" of divine abandonment in the affirmation of the second lines of verses 7 and 8. In the first lines of these two verses, as we have seen, the reality of God's abandonment of Israel is unambiguous. I read that as a way for us to think about our own season of virus as a time of God-abandonment, a reality that is experienced by many people.

Given the certitude of abandonment in the first lines of these two verses, we are not ready for the reversal that is voiced in the pair of second lines. Thus I want to consider the nature of that reversal that twice juxtaposes *divine abandonment* and *divine compassion*. The two negatives are "abandoned" and "hid my face." The two positives are twice "compassion." In the first case, compassion is intensified by the modifier "great," that is, immense in force. The consequence of that "great compassion" is "gathering," that is, homecoming to Jerusalem. "Compassion," moreover, is articulated in the plural, that is, compassion in abundance. In the second usage "compassion" is an active verb, "I will have compassion," and is modified by "everlasting fidelity" (*hesed*). Thus twice "compassion, once a verb, once a noun, both times intensified by a modifier. It is an assurance of homecoming, the end of exile, the reversal of historical fortunes.

Thus the two lines of *abandonment/compassion* are connected by an adversative conjunction (*waw*-consecutive) rendered as "but." Rhetorically the great reversal is accomplished by the conjunction. The rhetoric does not at all mind that the second line contradicts the first line; this usage of the conjunction is quite common in the rhetoric of Israel, especially in the wisdom tradition (see Prov 10:3, 4, 5, 6, for example).

My wonderment is how, beyond the obvious rhetorical maneuver, this great reversal is accomplished. (In our own historical context this reversal could be a reversal from the acute threat of virus to a virus-free historical prospect.) The usual scholarly way of understanding the reversal is that rhetoric simply follows historical sequence. Thus the two lines concerning "abandonment" reflect the displacement of Jews in Babylon (on which see Ps 137; Jer 52:28–30; Neh 1:4–8). Thus the poet, Isaiah, could give voice to the evident reality of displaced Jews that he rendered as divine absence. Conversely the two second lines reflect the momentous turn of history when Cyrus the Persian, defeated the Babylonians and introduced a new policy that permitted displaced peoples to return to their homelands (2 Chr 36:22–23). This historical outcome was clear enough that Isaiah could identify Cyrus as the Messiah of God, dispatched with God's intent for Jewish homecoming (see Isa 44:28; 45:1). The calculus is a quite ordinary one for our conventional interpretation:

abandonment = Babylonian displacement

compassion = Persian restoration

If we extend the calculus, we may reason this way:

abandonment = virus;

compassion = end of threat of virus

Rhetoric is led by historical experience. This characteristic rhetoric, moreover, permits God to be noticed and acknowledged in and through historical experience. These connections from *historical experience* through *rhetoric to theological affirmation* are conventional and unexceptional; they are also not very interesting.

But consider if we imagine for now that the rhetoric and theological claim are not led by historical events. What if we think, just for now, that historical experience is led by theological reality, that is, by the stunning reversal that takes place in God's own life. If we begin in this way, we may ask what is going on with *God* (here offered as a character persona) that could lead to such an *utterance* of reversal that would in turn lead to *historical reversal* and emancipation. Such reasoning would be like asking (just for now!) what could happen in the life of God that would lead to emancipation from the threat of the virus. This is, to be sure, an odd way of thinking in the modern world. It is nonetheless a way of thinking that belongs properly to the life of the church. What happens in *the life of God* that eventuates in *the life of the world*?

When we think in this way, we may ask, what is it that evoked God's stunning reversal from abandonment to compassion? Maybe the following is a response to such as query. I propose that in the midst of the displacement of exile God *heard* the laments of Israel; God *saw* the suffering of Israel; God *knew* the hard circumstance of Israel. . .all echoes of the beginning point of the Exodus narrative:

> After a long time the king of Egypt died. The Israelites groaned under their slavery, and cried out. Out of their slavery their cry for help rose up to God. God *heard* their groaning, and God *remembered* his covenant with Abraham, Isaac, and Jacob. God *looked upon* the Israelites, and God *took notice* of them. (Exod 2:23–25)

"God saw . . . God heard . . . God took notice"! And when God has heard and seen and took notice, God is moved by compassion for Israel. Thus God's compassion either: a) had been shelved by God's displeasure with Israel; or b) was not fully known by God until now, so that God reached out to depths of compassion that

or c) this passion cooled — he had been temporarily blinded by his anger

124

heretofore were not on God's screen. This latter would suggest that the dread historical experience of exile led God to new awareness and risk. *Mutatis mutandis*, we may hope or imagine that the extremity of the virus may lead to a like jolt in God's compassion.

We have some poetic renderings of the way in which the suffering of God's beloved evokes new compassion on the part of God. In Hosea 11:1–9 God reverses field as God reflects on obligations and commitments to beloved Israel:

> My heart recoils within me;
>> my *compassion* grows warm and tender.
> I will not execute my fierce anger . . . (vv. 8–9)

In Jeremiah 31:20 God finds that God is finally unable to "speak against my dear son."

> As often as I speak against him,
>> I still remember him.
> Therefore I am deeply moved for him;
>> I will surely have *mercy* on him, says the LORD.

The term rendered "mercy" in NRSV is the same word that is elsewhere "compassion"; the term here, moreover, is with an infinitive absolute for great intensification of the verb, "have mercy." And in Isaiah 49:15 God reaches into mother-love that leads to new historical possibility:

> Can a woman forget her nursing child,
>> or show no *compassion* for the child of her womb?
> Even these may forget,
>> yet I will not forget you.

The God evidenced in these poetic forays is not the settled God of philosophical ontology. This is God alive in the on-going drama of covenantal fidelity. In that drama, God may be moved by worldly engagement to find new dimensions of compassion. That has been the truth of the gospel narrative since God responded to the Hebrew slaves in Egypt. It is the truth of the gospel embodied in and enacted by Jesus, upon seeing the hungry crowd, was moved to compassion" (Mark 6:34; 8:2). The phrasing in the narrative suggests an internal disturbance in Jesus' digestive system when he saw the hungry folk. This is indeed bodily engagement! We may belatedly imagine that our context of virus will, in like manner, evoke a fresh measure of transformative attentiveness on God's part. It is the special burden of the church (and its preachers) to dig deeper into that covenantal reality that is the truth of our life, to probe into and imagine the stunning new reality of God's own life. The great reversal that Israel was able to live out is a reversal wrought in God's own life. The great reversal in God's own life is known among us since the Exodus wherein the suffering of the beloved opened new waves of historical possibility. This God is not so settled in divine splendor that there can be no fresh measure of God's best, most generous, most transformative capacity.

A loving God. A god who changes his mind

A god who listens and acts.

Flexible adaptable creative

— or at least such is our perception

— capable of being angry and

of being 'blinded' or at least not able

/ willing to change his mind for a while

19

Gratitude as Subversion

THANKSGIVING DAY, FOR ALL its entanglement with white violence against Native Americans, is a reminder to us that even in such a difficult time as this, gratitude is the hallmark of the Christian life. It is an acknowledgment that we are on the receiving end of life and it is the generous creator God who is on the giving end of our life. We may well linger over Paul's rhetorical question:

> What do you have that you did not receive? And if you have received it, why do you boast as if it were not a gift? (1 Cor 4:7)

The answer is "nothing!" We have nothing that we have not received as a gift. We have nothing durable that we treasure that we have devised, invented, produced or achieved; gratitude is responding back to God's limitless generosity, the one who gives good gifts to all of God's creatures,

We may especially notice that while gratitude is an attitude that marks all of our life in faith, gratitude also consists in regular specific disciplines. Psalm 107, a great model of thanksgiving, cites four cases of rescue for which the Psalmist is grateful:

desert hunger (vv. 4–9)
release from prison (vv. 12–16)
sickness (vv. 17–22), and
danger at sea (vv. 23–32).

In each instance, the speaker voice gives thanks back to God:

Let them thank the LORD for his steadfast love,
for his wonderful works to humankind. (vv. 8, 15, 21, 31)

In the third case, the matter of thanks is further exposited:

And led them offer *thanksgiving sacrifices,*
and *tell of his deeds* with songs of joy. (v. 22)

We learn that gratitude consists in: a) a *material offer of goods* (thanksgiving sacrifices!); and b) an *out loud narrative that recites the blessings* for which we give thanks, with an accent on specificity. That is, in the assembly of the faithful we "count our blessings." Regular *generous acts of materiality* and *narrative specificity* are gestures that keep us mindful that we are on the receiving end of limitless generosity.

If we fail in these disciplines, we can easily fall into the trap of imagining that we are on the initiating end of blessing the world. We can imagine that our worldly success is our achievement, and therefore our possession and therefore at our disposal for our own uses. In the transactional world all around us that lives by a, calculus of *quid pro quo* this leads some to imagine self-sufficiency that leads in turn to greed and eventually to predatory violence toward those who threaten our guarded surplus. That is the seduction of *pride* in our self-sufficiency and autonomy, eventually requiring awareness that we cannot finally sustain such an allusion. When we arrive at that awareness our pride readily turns to *despair;* we come to recognize that we cannot make our world safe and happy for ourselves. Thus the world of *quid pro quo* wavers *from pride to despair,* perhaps back to pride and again to despair. Gratitude is *the antidote to pride,* that life is not our achievement but a gift. This is not our world! Gratitude is the *antidote to despair* because in every circumstance we still live by gifts faithfully given.

Thus gratitude is a form of vigorous resistance against the seductions of the transactional world, empowering us to live apart from both pride and despair, apart from the toxic ideologies that beset our economy. Gratitude is the disciplined affirmation that the temptations of pride and despair are null and void and have no power over us.

I suggest that the hymn, "Now Thank We All Our God," the anthem of my tradition of German pietism, a welcome model for a life of disciplined gratitude.

> Now thank we all our God, with heart, and hands, and voices,
> who wondrous things hath done, in whom this world rejoices;
> who from our mother's arms hath blessed us on our way
> with countless gifts of love, and still is ours today.
> O may this bounteous God through all our life be near us!
> with ever joyful hearts and blessed peace to cheer us;
> and keep us in his grace and guide us when perplexed,
> and free us from all ills in this world and the next.
> All praise and thanks to God the Father now be given,
> the Son and him who reigns with them in highest heaven,
> eternal, Triune God, whom earth and heaven adore;
> for thus it was, is now, and shall be evermore.[1]

This warm intimate trusting poetry was written by Pastor Martin Rinkart as a table grace during the Thirty Years War that devastated all of Europe. His wife had died of the pestilence (read "virus!"?] and he wrote this for his children. The hymn affirms that we, along with Pastor Rinkart and his children, are on the receiving end of God's goodness even in the most dire circumstance.

This alternative way of being in the world, alternative to the common fear, greed, and violence that marks our public life, has immense practical implications for public life and public policy. It proposes, against both our pride and our despair, that public practice and public policy may be generous in the sharing of common resources with all of our neighbors and that we give up the posture of parsimony that defines so much of our common life.

1. *Prayer Book and Hymnal*, 396.

That "normal" parsimony is based on our tacit assumption of self-sufficiency that we have made it all and are entitled to it all, and on our "normal" despair that there is not enough to go around. Gratitude refuses both assumptions and declares such parsimony to be abnormal and out of sync with the reality of the creator who gives good gifts in abundance. Gratitude is an act of subversion that sees our neighbors as common recipients of the gifts given to us and through is to the neighbors. In missional and liturgical ways the church in its gratitude witnesses to "a more excellent way," a way that corresponds to God's good intention for God's world.

1 Cor 12 v 31
↪ 14 v 1

'Pursue love and strive for more spiritual gifts.'

20

Emancipation, Restoration, Homecoming

ALREADY IN THE LYRICAL affirmation of new (restored) creation after the chaos of the flood, Israel celebrated the regularity of creation as the various seasons follow reliably in sequence one after another:

> As long as the earth endures,
>   seedtime and harvest, cold and heat,
> summer and winter, day and night,
>   shall not cease. (Gen 8:22)

You can count on it! Farmers depend on it! Indeed the entire economy that must have food counts on that reliability without even thinking about it. Even in the midst of climate change (global weirdness!) the seasons follow one after another as witness to the governance of the creator.

Now in this lectionary snippet Isaiah appeals to that same reliable regularity (Isa 55:10). In this pre-scientific doxological awareness, the source of rain and snow is "from heaven," that is, from beyond human contrivance. Rain in the summer and snow in the winter bespeak the willingness of the creator to sustain the earth. The point is celebrated in the Book of Job:

Have you entered the storehouses of the snow,
    or have you seen the storehouses of the hail,
which I have reserved for the time of trouble,
    for the day of battle and war?
What is the way to the place where the light is distributed,
    or where the east wind is scattered in the earth?
Who has cut a channel for the torrents of rain,
    and a way for the thunderbolt,
to bring rain on a land where no one lives,
    on the desert, which is empty of human life,
to satisfy the waste and desolate land,
    and to make the ground put out forth grass?
(Job 38:22–27)

That which we take for granted is recognized in biblical faith as an awesome witness to the fidelity of the creator. It is this fidelity that is the elemental source of "seed and bread."

Isaiah makes appeal to this reliable regularity not for its own sake, but for a very different accent. As Isaiah 55:10 points to that *reliable regularity in creation*, so verse 11 points to a very different reliability, one that is as sure as that of creation. In verse 11 it is the word of God's mouth that is reliable. That word from God's mouth is performative; it does what it says. It is not idle chatter (empty). It is purposeful in the world. Thus the juxtaposition of verses 10 and 11 is the juxtaposition of *God in creation ("nature")* and *God in history*, in the affairs of the nations. The Bible always takes "creation and history" as twin distinct spheres of reality that share in the force of God's governance.

As a consequence we may ask what that word from the mouth of God purposes and promises. This claim of course contradicts all Enlightenment thinking that features a "turn to the subject" and wants to squeeze out God's governance or reduce God's work simply to that or "clock-maker." The prophetic tradition, however, has no doubt that God's purpose permeates and occupies the on-going processes of human history as it does the processes of creation. Mostly those purposes are recognized and known in retrospect; it is prophetic poetic work, however, to anticipate that out-working of God's purpose in history from what we know of God and what we know of God's past performance of purpose.

In the book of Isaiah, Second Isaiah in the exile begins in the chapter 40. In that chapter made famous by Handel's *Messiah*, the poet gives us access to a debate in the court of God as members of the court (angels, godlettes) ponder the rule of God. In this conversation it is conceded that the grass withers and the flower fades, that is, nothing in creation is finally durable. But then in 40:8 one voice asserts to the contrary that one thing lasts and does not wither or fade. God's word, God's purpose, God's declaration of rule is unlike withering grass or fading flower because that word does not wither or fade. It lasts forever!

The poet makes a stunning rhetorical maneuver. On the one hand the poet makes this *sweeping cosmic claim* for the decree as the sovereign rule of God. On the other hand, however, that word is given *specific historical fleshly content*. The great sovereign purpose of God is that the Jews in exile will return home from Babylon to Jerusalem. Thus in 55:11–13 the poet conjures a dramatic scene: "you"—you exiled people of God—shall go out (from Babylon) and be led back (to Jerusalem). "Joy and peace" will mark the journey home. It is a celebrative procession of homecoming. The Great Highway on which the returnees travel (see 40:3–5) will be lined with those who gather to cheer them home. Lined up to cheer are all the other creatures who also trust the good rule of God: the mountains, the hills, and the trees, the same cast of characters who in Psalm 96:11–12 applauded the kingship of God. The image we get is not unlike that of the corridors of a hospital lined with medical personnel cheering those recovering from the virus on their way home with a prospect of restored health. The returnees from exile are like that, cheered on their way home into recovery and wellbeing.

For all the grand lyric of the poem, we should not miss the astonishing historical import of the poetry. This poetic utterance is offered while the Babylonian empire is still the master of estrangement for these displaced Jews to whom the poetry is addressed. In prophetic imagination that refuses to give in to Babylon, the word of God outruns and contradicts the will of the Babylonian empire. The purpose of God overrides all other sovereignty. And now that divine will is put to work on behalf of the emancipation of the Jews who had been held helpless and impotent by Babylon. No one could have anticipated such an *emancipation* and no one could have hoped for such a *restoration*. Given this historical horizon of Babylon, emancipation and homecoming are impossible. The point of the poetry, however, is that the word of God does what the world judges to be impossible in order to restore to wellbeing those whom God loves.

The preacher need only extend this deep counter-truth, with specificity, to our own time, place, and circumstance. The preacher is always to assert the good news of God in circumstances of crisis that are closed down, hopeless, and in despair. This means, every time, that the resolve of God

> opens what is closed down,
>> hopes against hopelessness,
>>> overrides despair in resolve, and
>>>> makes all things new!

The poet does not explain; it is not the work of the poet to explain. Nor is it the work of the preacher. The poet and the preacher proclaim the counter-truth among us so as to expose the false claims of fear, scarcity, and greed that cannot withstand the word of God. This counter-truth is variously addressed concerning:

—*the poor* who are locked into poverty
—*the wealthy* who are sated by commodity
—*people of color* who suffer exclusion
—*white people* who are locked into fear
—*all of us* amid the virus.

The news is that there is a word at work among us from beyond us, "sent from heaven above" that is as reliable as rain, as regular as snow. The church has seen this transformative word fleshed in Jesus. No wonder he dazzled the people (Matt 7:28–29). And no wonder he had to be executed because he threatened the certitudes of the fearful. Pharaoh, Caesar, and the National Security State always have it all buttoned down, made safe and secure for the privileged. The narrative entrusted to us, however, is the news of emancipation from the force of greed, fear, and violence that cannot finally prevail because the word of God is at work in the world. That word is a wedge of newness in a world seemingly closed. That word evokes human energy and recruits human courage for the endless work of *emancipation, restoration,* and *homecoming.* Once human agency embraces that sovereign word, the juices of wellbeing are set loose in the world! That is why the next verse in Isaiah after the glorious procession home speaks of the maintenance of justice that is genuinely human work (Isa 56:1)!

Bibliography

Baptist, Edward E. *The Half Has Never Been Told: Slavery and the Story of American Capitalism*. New York: Basic Books, 2016.

Baradan, Mehra. *The Color of Money: Black Banks and the Racial Wealth Gap*. Cambridge, MA: Belnap, 2017.

Barth, Karl. *Church Dogmatics*. Vol. I, *The Doctrine of the Word of God*, Part 2: ed. T. F. Torrance; ed. and G. W. Bromiley. Translated by G. W. Bromiley, G. T. Thomson, and Harold Knight. Edinburgh: T. & T. Clark, 1956.

———. *Church Dogmatics*. Vol. IV, *The Doctrine of Reconciliation, Part 1*. Edited by G. W. Bromiley and T. F. Torrance. Translated by G. W. Bromiley. Edinburgh: T. & T. Clark, 1956.

Beckert, Sven. *Empire of Cotton: A Global History*. New York: Knopf, 2014.

Block, Peter, Walter Brueggemann, and John McKnight. *An Other Kingdom: Departing the Consumer Society*. Hoboken, NJ: Wiley, 2016.

Boer, Roland. *The Sacred Economy of Ancient Israel*. Library of Ancient Israel. Louisville: Westminster John Knox, 2015.

Bradley, James. *The Imperial Cruise: A Secret History of Empire and War*. New York: Little, Brown, 2009.

Brown, Peter. *Through the Eye of a Needle: Wealth, the Fall of Rome, and the Making of Christianity in the West, 350–550 AD*. Princeton: Princeton University Press, 2013.

Brueggemann, Walter. *Journey to the Common Good*. Updated ed. Louisville: Westminster John Knox, 2021.

Buber, Martin. *The Eclipse of God: Studies in the Relation between Religion and Philosophy*. New York: Harper, 1952.

Caparrós, Martin. *Hunger: The Oldest Problem*. Translated by Katherine Silver. Rev. ed. Brooklyn: Melville, 2019.

Crüsemann, Frank. *The Torah: Theology and Social History of Old Testament Law*. Translated by Allan W. Mahnke. Minneapolis: Fortress, 1996.

Desmond, Matthew. *Evicted: Poverty and Profit in the American City*. New York: Crown, 2016.

Bibliography

Dussel, Enrique D. *Ethics of Liberation: In the Age of Globalization and Exclusion.* Translated by Eduardo Mendieta. Edited by Alejandro A. Vallega. Latin America Otherwise. Durham: Duke University Press, 2013.

Ehrlich, Paul. *The Population Bomb.* Rev. ed. New York: Ballentine, 1971.

Ellison, Ralph. *Going to the Territory.* New York: Random House, 1986.

Fretheim, Terence E. *Glory to God.* Louisville: Westminster John Knox, 2013.

———. *God and the World in the Old Testament: A Relational Theology.* Nashville: Abingdon, 2005.

———. *The Suffering of God.* Overtures to Biblical Theology. Philadelphia: Fortress, 1984.

Glory to God. Louisville: Westminster John Knox, 2013.

Grant, Madison. *The Passing of the Great Race: or, The Racial Basis of European History.* New ed., revised and amplified, with a new preface by Henry Fairfield Osborn. New York: Scribner, 1916.

Harden, Garrett. "The Tragedy of the Commons." *Science* 162 (13 December 1968) 1243–48.

Lockwood, Frank E. "Bill by Senator Tom Cotton Targets Curriculum on Slavery." *Arkansas Democrat Gazette*, July 26, 2020. https://www.arkansasonline.com/news/2020/jul/26/bill-by-cotton-targets-curriculum-on-slavery/.

Lowell, James Russell. "The Present Crisis." In *Poems: Second Series*. Boston: Mussey, 1848.

Mantel, Hilary. *Wolf Hall: A Novel.* New York: Holt, 2009.

Moltmann, Jürgen. *The Crucified God: The Cross of Christ as the Foundation and Criticism of Christian Theology.* Translated by Margaret Kohl. 1974. Reprint, Minneapolis: Fortress, 1993.

Prayer Book and Hymnal. New York: Church Publishing Inc., 1985.

Russell, Mary Doria. *A Thread of Grace: A Novel.* New York: Random House, 2005.

Scott, James C. *Against the Grain: A Deep History of the Earliest States.* New Haven: Yale University Press, 2017.

Shah, Sonia. *The Next Great Migration: The Beauty and Terror of Life on the Move.* New York: Barnes & Noble, 2020.

Sonderegger, Katherine. *Systematic Theology.* Vol. 1, *The Doctrine of God.* Minneapolis: Fortress, 2015.

Spiro, Jonathan Peter. *Defending the Master Race: Conservation, Eugenics, and the Legacy of Madison Grant.* Burlington: University of Vermont Press, 2009.

Williams, Eric. *Capitalism & Slavery.* 1944. Reprint, Chapel Hill: University of North Carolina Press, 1994.

Zinn, Howard. *A People's History of the United States: 1492–Present.* New ed. New York: HarperCollins, 2003.

Index of Scripture

Index of Scripture

≈

Hebrews

Revelation

Index of Names

Index of Names

Lightning Source UK Ltd.
Milton Keynes UK
UKHW011243080722
405575UK00003B/752